Old Testament Lore

Old Testament Lore

A Mosaic Tapestry

NORMAN M. CHANSKY

RESOURCE *Publications* · Eugene, Oregon

OLD TESTAMENT LORE
A Mosaic Tapestry

Copyright © 2011 Norman Chansky. All rights reserved. Except for brief quotations in critical publications or reviews, no part of this book may be reproduced in any manner without prior written permission from the publisher. Write: Permissions, Wipf and Stock Publishers, 199 W. 8th Ave., Suite 3, Eugene, OR 97401.

Resource Publications
An Imprint of Wipf and Stock Publishers
199 W. 8th Ave., Suite 3
Eugene, OR 97401

www.wipfandstock.com

ISBN 13: 978-1-61097-010-5

Manufactured in the U.S.A.

To my children: Linda, James, Keren, Tamar, and Matthew

and to their children Elizabeth, Sara, Bethany, Gilad, Kinneret, Allison, Isaac, Meredith, Raia, and Emma

and to my great grandchild Daniella

and to my sisters: Lois and Sonya.

Words are inadequate to describe my appreciation to my wife Elissa for her support and inspiration.

Poetry is the suggestion by the imagination of noble grounds for noble emotions.

—John Ruskin,: *Modern Painters* III, iv. 1

Contents

Foreword xi

Preface xv

List of Abbreviations xvii

Chapter One The Pentateuch 1

Chapter Two The Prophets 113

Chapter Three The Writings 201

Chapter Four The Apocrypha 239

Foreword

Humans have always wondered about the mysteries of the universe as well as the unique history of their people. They ask what does my world consist of? How did it come about? They also seek to understand themselves, to know their personal stories, to find their place in the universe. Ancestors shaped their outlook on life;. humans wish to know how. For many of us the answer begins with Creation and continues through The Flood, the Patriarchs, and the Prophets.

However, each culture has its own creation story to fix its place in history and to define its destiny. It is hard to find a culture that does not evoke the divine. That story gives a culture its unique signature. According to a Crow Indian legend, in the beginning there was only water and ducks. Then the Sun, the Creator, merged with the Coyote. The Creator told the ducks to dive into the water and from the mud on their webbed feet the Earth was created and peopled. Early Egyptians explained that dry land appeared out of a primordial ocean. Atum, the Sun god- later named Ra, father of all other gods, arose from an abyss. In Mesopotamia, creation also took place from a watery abyss, Apsu. But the world came into being from a violent clash between older and younger gods. Marduk, made the sky and earth from two halves of the body of Tiamat, a dragon personifying evil. In Persian cosmology, Ahura Mazda was the creator of Man as well as the decider and ruler of natural events such as the course of the moon. Good and Evil, twin attributes of his character, contend for supremacy. In the end virtue defeats evil. The gods of the Greek and Roman pantheons go by the names of Zeus and Jupiter respectively. But neither were creators. Rather according to Greek mythology the world begins with Chaos, a vast void surrounded by water, the domain of Eurynome, the goddess of all things. She coupled with a snake and gave birth to Eros.

Eurynome separated the sky from the sea. Out of that relationship was born Gaia, Mother Earth, and Uranus, the Heavens. Gaia married Uranus and gave birth to the Titans, the most important of which was Cronus who married Rhea but then swallowed all of their children. Only Zeus survived by a trick devised by Gaia.

Compare these stories with an aboriginal creation myth. In the beginning all was still. All of the spirits of the earth were asleep. Then the Father of all Spirits stirred and woke up the Sun Mother who was bidden to go down to earth and awaken all of the spirits. Her light spread across the earth, melted ice which became oceans, rivers, and lakes. She penetrated into caves and wakened insects. These in turn combined with flowers of every color imaginable. She enjoined all creatures in the cosmos to live in peace with one another. Then she returned to the sky.

In sharp contrast is the Hebrew story of Creation. There is only one God Who Created the cosmos, by fiat, through words not brutality, trickery, or coaxing. "Let there be light!" This is how the Creation account of the Hebrews begins. Although the heavens and earth were Created from an abyss, it was the Spirit of God that Hovered over the deep dividing light from darkness. God is in complete control of the Creative process: day, night, vegetation, lower animals and higher animals. Man is Created with the mandate to protect all manner of life. Then on the seventh day God Rested and Gave the Sacred Sabbath to humanity. The Sacred Sabbath is also a Mandate.

Genesis is said to present two accounts of Creation: the P or priestly account (Gen I and II, 1–4) and the J account (Gen II 4b-24). There are several differences between them. In the former God is called "Elohim"; in the latter, the ineffable name *yood, hay, vav, hay* is sometimes transliterated "Yahweh." In the former, animals were Created before Man; in the latter, after Man. In the former, man and woman were Created simultaneously; in the latter, woman was taken from Adam's rib. These dual accounts are not isolated instances but templates for other narrations. There are multiple versions of the same "event" giving The Bible an aura of the recondite. Reconciling the versions and finding the deeper meanings of single accounts has been an undertaking of scholars of many faith communities for many centuries. Scholars extract meaning through the special blueprint that charts their courses. All readers delve into the sacred text and map their own meanings in an effort to define who were their ancestors, who they are now and who they seek to become.

Our knowledge of the past is ever expanding; the meanings we derive from the Old Testament, therefore, alter as well.

Preface

THE LURE AND LORE of The Old Testament is magnetic. The aim of this book of poetry is to draw the reader to its lodestone. Extracting the universal essences of that holy book, this collection of poems maps the journey into the spine and soul of the people of The Old Testament as they grew up. Imagine that we gather at the base of the mystical Mount Sinai, rampart against idolatry. Overhead is a canopy of sundry inspired images, rhymes, and rhythms. All sacred; all hallowed. Stitched into that canopy is a rich saga of a people struggling to remain alive, to achieve some semblance of dignity, and to transmit God's Message from the holy mount. Resisting memory's urge to fade and forget, the words of the Old Testament live on, electrify, intrigue, and enchant us with their grandeur. Old Testament Lore accesses treasured biblical sagas through poesy. It does not retell history but it imaginatively renders the biblical narrative. Included herein are poems that ignite mystery and awe since the dawn of Creation. Witness the struggles, feats, foibles, sapience, and ardor of Adam and his descendants, including Noah and Abraham and their lines, during halcyon and stormy times. Plumb the words of the poets and prophets. Sing their songs.

Most of the poems in this work were prompted by books of the Jewish canon: The Pentateuch, Prophets, and the Writings. A few poems were inspired by the Apocrypha, writings in the Old Testament style, which are sacred to some faith communities but not all. The four chapters in this collection correspond to the above cited four books. In writing the poems I used a number of styles found in Biblical texts: rhyme, rhythm, alliteration, assonance, metonymy, simile, and parallelism. The plan of this collection is to begin poems with my liberal adaptation of a Biblical reference in *italics*.

Readers are invited to view the biblical narrative through my lens and reflect them through their prism. The Bible is like a kaleidoscope, a treasure trove of many shapes and colors wandering about in a cylinder, in arrangements that captivate, in patterns which fascinate, reflecting motifs geometric, harmonious and symmetric. No matter the design one beholds, a people of beauty poignantly unfolds.

Norman M. Chansky, PhD

List of Abbreviations

Gen	Genesis
Exod	Exodus
Jdt	Judith
Num	Numbers
Wis	Wisdom of Solomon
Deut	Deuteronomy
Sir	Sirach
Josh	Joshua
Bar	Baruch
Judg	Judges1–3
Esd	Esdras
Ruth	Ruth
Ep Jer	Letter of Jeremiah
1–2 Sam	Samuel
Sg Three	Song of Three Young Men
1–2 Kgs	Kings
Sus	Susanna
1–2 Chr	Chronicles
Bel	Bel and the Dragon
Ezra	Ezra1–2
Macc	Maccabees
Neh	Nehemia
Pr Man	Prayer if Manasseh
Esth	Esther
Tob	Tobias
Job	Job
Ps	Psalm
Prov	Proverbs

Eccl	Ecclesiastes
Song	Song of Solomon
Isa	Isaiah
Jer	Jeremiah
Lam	Lamentations
Ezek	Ezekiel
Dan	Daniel
Hos	Hosea
Joel	Joel
Amos	Amos
Obad	Obadiah
Jonah	Jonah
Mic	Micah
Nah	Nahum
Hab	Habbakuk
Zeph	Zephania
Hag	Haggai
Zech	Zechariah
Mal	Malachi

1 The Pentateuch

THE FIRST SEVEN DAYS: VERSION ONE

In the beginning God Created heaven and earth. The earth was unformed and dark. The Spirit of God Encircled the earth. And God Said "Let there be light." And there was light. And God Saw that the light was good. Then God Separated the light from the darkness. And there was evening and morning on the first day. Gen I, 1-4. The earth was filled with water and God Made a Celestial Sphere and Separated waters beneath it and above it. God Called The Celestial Sphere "Heaven." The second day ended. On the third day God Separated the waters beneath the Celestial Sphere and Called the dry land "Earth" which generated grasses, herbs, and all manner of trees. On the fourth day the Celestial Lights (the sun, the moon, the stars, the planets) issued forth to illume the night and to mark the seasons. On the fifth day all manner of creatures inhabited the earth. On the sixth day God Created Humans to be merciful caretakers of Creation. On the seventh day, after all was finished, God Rested and Declared it Sabbath Ordained a holy day, to be kept every week as a joyous day of rest. Gen I, 6 ff.

Day 1. In the Beginning there was The Sacred Source,
    Within which God, Perfect and Without Equal Exists.
From that Source endless, dark, multicolored, formless space
    Arose and silently stretched its vastness
And returned to surround the Sacred Source.
    Then did God Bless the expanding space.

God Exists in Space and Space reflects God's Infinity.

Day 2. Then gasses formed and mixed rising vapors and prisms.
    Then God Gathered clusters of gasses

And Cradled them and Pressed them closely and lovingly
> Until multicolored fires ignited

And Scattered them to give birth to orbs of suns and stars.
> And the stars released oxygen into the cosmos.

Each heavenly light shone God's Dazzling Radiance and spread God's Thermonuclear Warmth.
> Then did God Bless the suns and stars and all astral generations.

Then did each fiery orb release many kinds of dust, each with its own electrical charges.
> Some dusts drifted aimlessly; others slammed into one another and formed mass;

Some hardened into rocks; others melted into rivers of metal.

*God Exists in suns, stars, sands, rocks
and they reflect God's Creative Fires.*

Day 3. Then God Gathered and Combined emerging gasses and dusts
> And Formed planets, each with its own distance from the Sun;

Each with its own motion:
> Each with its own orbit according to an ordained schedule.

No planet falling; no planet failing; each held in place by gravity.
> Then were the planets and their seasons Blessed

For they were all good to God.

God Exists in planets whose rhythm reflect God's Peerless Design.

Day 4. Gasses spread and surrounded the Earth planet,
> Admitting Light so that Creation's Works could be seen

Yet providing a protective shield to the eyes
> And allowing warmth to pass through the atmosphere

While protecting all creatures from burning.
> The Sun tended the spinning Earth by day and the moon by night.

Newly emerging gasses collided, separated and broke away
> And recombined to form seas where life would flourish.

And gasses rising from the seas united with other elements to form air for breathing.

Moving land masses collided to make mountains rise from the
    seas
Hiding minerals beneath the great depths.
    Then did God Bless the Earth planet and all planets yet to be born
    in the cosmos.

*God Exists in all planets whose seas, atmosphere, and hills
reflect God's Heights and Depths.*

Day 5. Proteins, dusts, sodium, zinc, ammonia, cesium, and cobalt
    drifted idly.
    Then God Mixed these elements with ocean sprays and Whirled
    them in Mystic Broth.
Then Did God Make an ocean vent rise and warm the salty broth
    Until the elements coalesced.
And then there was Life.
    Bacteria. Cells.
Mitochondria! Messengers of God!
    Then did God Create amino acids: adenine, thymine, cytosine,
    and guanine.
Then did God Twist the helix of amino acids and Rearrange them in
    infinite patterns,
    Bridging them with sugars and phosphates in spiraling ladders.
The emerging proteins became the endless fonts of life.
    Mitochondria, attaching themselves to mothers' generative cells,
Energized the helix.
    Then did God's Messengers Breathe life into the generative cells
And Gave each creature a sacred voice and a sacred cadence for all
    time.
    And God Choreographed life on Earth
With crawling animals and walking animals;
    There were fruit trees for fruit eaters;
There were nut trees for nut eaters;
    Herbivores and carnivores; procreators and scavengers.
Parasites, epiphytes and symbionts.
    Each absorbed God; each extended the Divine Genius of Creation.
Then there appeared all manner of flora:

> Those to grow in the sea, those to grow in the air, those to grow on the land.
>
> Those that flower, those that bring forth fruit; those that bear nuts.
>> Those that are eaten; those that are merely admired.
>
> Those that complete their cycle in one season;
>> Those that survive for centuries.
>
> Firs with needles; cacti with thorns; trees with leaves;
>> Each plant producing its own kind for all generations;
>
> Each plant transmitting its seeds to carry on its species;
>> Each seed unfolding new and unique qualities;
>
> Each seed mixing with others of the same species to build a new family.
>> New combinations of proteins brought forth all manner of fauna.
>
> Insects that crawl and those that fly.
>> All manner of birds were brought forth.
>
> Those that float; those that fly; and those that walk on land.
>> All manner fish were brought forth:
>
> Those that swim and those that crawl on the sea bottom.
>> All manner of animals were brought forth:
>
> Those living in caves; those living in trees; and those living in the wild.
>> Those that are fleet; those that are slow-footed.
>
> Then did God Bless the plants and the animals
>> And all life bearing chromosomes for the next generation.

> *God's Genius Exists in flora and fauna*
> *and they reflect God's Living Infinite Presence.*

Day 6. After Careful Meditation
> God's Genius Rearranged spiraling amino acids, phosphates and sugars.

Each new helical twist brought forth a different human family:
> The tall, the short; the dark, the light; the narrow, the stout.

Each was Endowed with The Holy Spirit; each was Selected to protect Nature.
> Each was Selected to discover order in and extend the unfolding worlds of Nature.

Each was Selected to bring order to the worlds of Nature.

Each was Selected with the intelligence to study Nature's secrets.
Each was Fitted with the power to preserve and extend Creation.
> Each was Fitted with the choice of conserving Nature or destroying it.

Within each human God Inscribed the Sacred Knowledge of Right and Wrong
> To balance destructive, generative, and protective impulses.

To each new generation Was Revealed Nature known since antiquity;
> To each new generation Was Revealed Nature unknown to its forbears.

Each human Was Given the power to reason, enhance, and intensify thought.
> Each human Was Given power to construct and reflect.

Each human Was Given the sparks of Mercy and Forgiveness;
> Each human Was Given the resolve to serve others through Sacred Inspirations.

To God each human is holy; no one is more treasured than another.
> Each is a scion of the Sacred Source.

When the systems were in place for all Creation to be good for all Time,
> God Blessed the human families and Assigned them the duty to protect Creation.

God's Grace Exists in human families
and human families reflect God's Greatness and Infinity.

Day 7. When the patterns of Nature were completed, God Rested and Found Peace.
> So it was with heavenly hosts circling for eternity:
>> a time to give light, a time to renew.

So it is with the seas which rage today and whisper in the morrow.
> So it is with the trees which awake in Summer and sleep in Winter.

So it is with all manner of life, seeking food and shelter for days
> Then resting to prepare for the next quest.

So it is with God in glittering glory and with Ardor Created the cosmos in six days
> And Rested on the seventh to Contemplate on its wonders and Remember them.

God Ordained that humans work six days and restore themselves on the seventh, the Sabbath.
Since that First Day of Rest has God Blessed each Sabbath day and Made it Sacred.

*God's Glory Glitters in cycles of Creation and Rest
and Exists in all of Nature.*

And all of Nature Reflects Harmoniously Rhythmic Continuity.

THE FIRST SEVEN DAYS: VERSION TWO[1]

Within each particle throughout the Vast
    That had no present and had no past
Dwelled God, Enshrined in endless Time,
    Circled by depths and heights sublime.

All was hot and dark and still,
    When swiftly dawned The Creator's Will,
Launching lightning in all directions,
    Pursued by thunder's ricocheting reflections.

It was then that Time began
    And when Space, as well, spread its span.
Light eddied from a fiery sun
    And rings of planets in the cosmos spun.

Distant stars, jewels of the night,
    Watched Earth born 'midst showers of Light.
Gasses mixed and moisture spread
    And living matter then was bred.

From the waters seas had formed,
    Washed the world and brewed the storm.
Then Baptized cells as they arrived,
    Nourished them, too, and they survived.

Plants grew up, both short and tall,
    With flowers and fruits that ever enthrall.
Mountains rose to majestic size
    Reaching high to the swelling skies.

Families of fish swarmed the seas
    Spreading rainbow fantasies.
Animals roved the land to find
    The havens which God to them Assigned.

    1. Paralleling the two versions of the Creation story in the Bible

Birds in the sky would daily scout
    Nesting places all about.
Each bird chirped its very own song,
    And animals and trees sang along.

Plainly lacking was a human pair
    To tend to all with loving care.
Moments after Divine Meditation,
    Humans arose to crown Creation.

Woman and Man, God Created
    With both limitless love and hate unabated .
Adam, the man, and Eve, the wife,
    Were placed on Earth to honor life.

To their souls God Conveyed
    The laws of decency to be obeyed
Plants and animals with loving kindness to be tended
    And Nature's frail were by humans to be mended.

God Ordained, when all was done,
    A Sabbath day, a holy one,
A day of prayer, a day of rest,
    A day Eternal God Had Blessed.

SABBATH IS AN EDEN

And God Blessing the seventh day Made it holy. That day was Ordained a day of rest from all that was Created. Gen II, 3.

Sabbath is an Eden away from the noisy crowds;
    Where Voices soft are heard of Angels beyond the clouds.
And where the eyes watch daffodils gilding a Sacred mound;
    Where sweet attar of roses is in every whiffet found.
And where ambrosia flavors every food and kindles a savor of taste;
    Where every thought the mind devises is wise, uplifting, and chaste.
And where each heart is beating with the rhythm of Creation;
    Where every soul is set to worship God in adoration.
At that moment our hands join with those who have gone before;
    At that moment generations to come will join with those of yore.
And every wounded soul will heal from Eden's Soothing Balm
    And will be rendered into words of a sacred Sabbath psalm.

QUEST TO SURMISE NATURE'S ASPECTS: Two Haiku Poems

Complexity

The weave of Nature
    Is spun silky and gritty
In knots and tangles.

Indefinable Creation

Mystery and chance
    Play dice with the universe
And scoff at Science.

BLESSED ARE THEY WHO SEEK GOD IN EVERY GENE

Blessed are they who seek God
    In every gene
And reveal its mystery.

THE FIRST HUMANS: VERSION ONE

God Said: "Let us Fashion a human in our image, a version of OurSelves. Gen I, 26.

God Sought the counsel of Angels, partners in Causation.
  "Let a race of human creatures crown Creation;
A race who will respect My Authority
  And preserve and augment Creation's immensity."
The Consenters advised, "Create a creature
  With a Mind like Yours capable of learning,
  With a Soul like Yours sprouting righteousness,
  With a Heart like Yours overflowing with mercy."
The Dissenters advised, "such a creature
  Would have a mind abounding in ignorance,
  Would have a spirit sprouting wrong doing,
  Would have a heart flowing with malice.
  What creature can be as perfect as God?
But God Accepted the advice of the Consenters.
  "You will rue this day," scoffed the Dissenters!
In a thrice some genes in God's laboratory mutated
  And from the Essence of God were fashioned humans: Men and Women,
Not too many, as humanity was still an experiment.
  Adam and Eve, closest to God in mind, soul, and heart were endowed with free will.
God said, "live upon My Creation, enjoy it, improve upon it
  But you must be obedient and be responsible for your actions."
God placed them side by side in The Garden of Eden, Epicenter of Creation,
  And consecrated their marriage, pronouncing them husband and wife.
Each was the complement of the other; each the help mate of the other.
  A choir of the Consenters filled the heavens with sweet songs
Which wafted out of The Garden and is heard today in the arias of the birds.
  The hearts of the newlyweds were filled with rapture.

But the vexed Dissenters brewed cannons of thunder which rumble even today.
    The newlyweds sought shelter from the tantrums of the Dissenters.
Rain drowned their ecstasy.
    In time Adam and Eve learned what hunger is and how to satisfy it,
What thirst is and how to slake it, what heat and cold are and how to protect their bodies.
    What beauty is and how to admire it;
What comfort is and how to enjoy it.
    What knowledge is and how to increase it.
They learned how to make babies:
    How to feed them, protect them, and how to teach them to survive.
But they also discovered need, greed, and evil.
    They surrendered to temptations and engaged in actions Scorned by God.
They disobeyed as well as God's Forgiveness but also exile from Paradise.
    The refugees learned about the work of life and the permanence of death.
They built houses protecting them from the elements and fortifying them from foes;
    They sewed garments shielding their skin.
They composed songs celebrating God's Creation; they painted visions of history.
    They witnessed murder and learned to grieve, to console, and to endure.
They taught their lessons to their descendants and to other humans in God's Creation.
    And the Consenters who advised God to Create humans were vindicated

    And so were the Dissenters.

THE FIRST HUMANS: VERSION TWO

The biota of Eden were thriving
    And daily new species were arriving.
Blooms were on every manner of plant:
    Fruit bearing and flowers that enchant.

Stripe´d animals with great speed were running
    Leather-hided animals stretched out were sunning
Spotted animals through brush were leaping
    Night time animals lay in tree branches sleeping.

Birds nesting in all kinds of trees
    Were chirping entrancing melodies;
And fish were swimming hither and yon:
    Catch a glimpse and then they are gone.

Angels on high, God's Adjutants—Planners, Designers, and
    Confidantes
Marveled at the roots of God's Creation,
    The Very Cause of Cosmic Causation.

But as they Gazed upon the works they'd Schemed;
    Something was missing to Them it seemed.
Lacking was a bridge to God Above:
    A force of wisdom, of justice, of love

Who could preserve the Creation that was Wrought.
    Someone who would forge links, they sought,
Between the Sacred and the norm:
    Someone who would Creation transform.

For many eons at length they Debated
    And for many more they Meditated.
Finally they Developed a strategy
    And Formed a plan to which all could agree:

Simians were charming and clever as well
    And at solving problems did they excel.
Let us take an ovum from the primate, the very best,
    Mutate it, and then with Divine Seed invest.

In a Sacred amniotic stream the Angels Immersed
    Themselves and their imperfections were Dispersed.
At the moment that they were Purified,
    The spirit of God in them would Abide.

Seeds of life from the Angelic race
    Sped toward the ovum in a random pace.
When the seed and the ovum at last had met
    The two curtsied and whirled in a minuet.

Then one seed to the ovum was invited
    And the two gametes were united.
A zygote Divinely human was spun
    And what had been two now was one

Absorbed into an Angel's womb
    A human creature began to bloom.
Nurtured by the Sacred Water
    The human would become God's first daughter.

Surrounding the ovum in empyrean mystique
    The Angels Watched the fetus grow week by week.
Then after what seemed liked an interminable time
    Out of its nest a human did climb.

Its body somewhat resembled the chimpanzee
    But its soul was kin to The Deity.
The babe who from a labyrinth had crawled
    Was someone whom the Angels Enthralled.

When the woman was fully grown,
    The Radiance of God upon her shone.
Her fingers were agile, her posture was erect,
    Her brain was of superior intellect.

She was Eve, exuding life and cheer,
    Ready to conquer every new frontier.
From her celestial abode
    Along sacred waters she strode

Until she reached heaven's gate
    Which opened to Eden's utopian estate.
There she beheld a sylvan wonder,
    Opaque lightning and silent thunder.

There was Warmth to bathe her soft skin
    And Mercy to nourish her soul within.
When she would taste any manner of food,
    She blessed God in thankful mood.

But lonely she was and lonely she'd be;
    What kind of companion is a gnarled olive tree?
She petitioned the Angels to Send her a friend
    To be her husband with whom she would blend.

The Angels Set out to create a HE
    That would complement Eve, the living SHE.
In the sacred amniotic stream Angels again submerged
    And their imperfections again were purged.

At the moment that they were purified
    The spirit of God in them did Abide.
Then from another simian an ovum was extracted
    That to the Divine Seed would be attracted.

Seeds of life from the Angelic race
    Sped toward the ovum in a random pace.
When the seed and the ovum at last had met
    They curtsied and whirled in a minuet.

The two gametes were united
    When a seed to the ovum had been invited.
Again a zygote divinely human was spun
    And what had been two now was one.

Absorbed in an Angel's Merciful Womb
    A human creature began to bloom.
What a remarkable deed the Angel had Done
    And the human grew into a God's first son.

Erect like Eve with a comparable brain
    He was ready to explore the Divine Domain.
He wandered until he reached heaven's gate
    Which opened to Eden's utopian estate.

He looked about and was struck by awe
    And gave a name to whatever he saw.
Then in a stream he beheld his reflection
    And noticed that he had a reddish complexion.

From the language that he had improvised
    The sound "Adam" he then verbalized.
To him "Adam" meant "red,"
    The color he saw upon his head.

Wherever he traveled, wherever he went
    When he saw God's Creation he said "excellent."
He wandered for many a week;
    Then one morning he heard a shriek.

He was as frightened as was Eve,
    Another human to perceive.
A sound from his throat was then unchained
    Which would not ever be regained.

It was amazing; a beguiling mystery
    And the beginning of history:
Once an act is dispatched and done
    Its memory is stored and lingers on.

He remembered the shriek as did she
    And HE and SHE then became WE.
Each lonely creature reached for the other
    And walked hand in hand like sister and brother.

The mystery of voice was tantalizing
    And they spent many days speech analyzing.
Together they attached meaning to each uttered sound:
    For events mundane, for adventures profound.

Together they would taste the rain,
    Watch the moon on the wane.
Together they were awed by the golden sun,
    And chirped with the birds just for fun.

They climbed the branches of the linden tree
    Whose heart shaped leaves were poetry.
But the simian branches, now in the dozens,
    Evoked tenderness and joy in their human cousins.

They gamboled like deer from place to place
    And copied the gorilla in fond embrace.
Colors Eve saw in poignant hues:
    Ambers, crimsons, and azure blues.

These were the colors of the fire on the hill
    Which they daily watched just for the thrill.
One day they put a squash inside the heat
    And found the squash warm and tasty to eat.

They discovered what else can be done by the fire:
    Melt things, fuse things, and make wet things drier.
Every day was another epiphany,
    Revealing God's Creative Supremacy.

There was so much to learn of God's Sacred Plan
    By Eve, the woman, and Adam, the man.
Adding words to their vocabularies
    Blessed Creation's awesome Mysteries.

How fragrant was the bed of spices
    Step nearby and it entices
Each to taste the cinnamon, curry, thyme, and cloves
    And to learn how to grow such treasure troves.

Their ears were filled with all kinds of sounds.
    Like the crying of cats, the yelping of hounds
Whispering trees, and palm fronds clacking,
    Hands clapping, wet lips smacking.

Birds chirping; stomachs burping,
    Horses neighing; donkeys braying.
Lions roaring; ruminants bleating;
    Water pouring, elephants eating.

Adam blew wind into the horn of a ram
    Trumpeting a sound that awakened his lamb.
Eve cut thickets and twisted their vines
    And decorated Eden in exquisite designs.

The Sun shone by day warming the land;
> At night Moon and Stars glowed by God's Command.

Day was the time to learn and see;
> Night was the time for ecstasy.

They gathered old leaves into a heap
> And lay upon them preparing to sleep.

Adam reached for Eve's curly hair,
> Smoother than silk and twisted with flair.

His fingers lingered on her swanlike neck
> And his tongue licked a speck

Of pollen from an apple tree
> That had been overlooked by a honey bee.

Eve placed her hand upon Adam's head
> And ran it through his hair of red.

Adam caressed Eve's little ear
> And kissed her eye trickling a tear.

At long last their mouths invented the kiss
> And then they discovered the meaning of bliss.

The evening was cool and both trembled with chill;
> They embraced one another and twisted with thrill.

They quivered;
> They shivered.

Their hearts skipped a beat
> And soaring in both were surges of heat.

Their love reached higher than the linden tree's crown
> Whose trunk was softer than eider down.

The two warm bodies combined as one
> And what was begun could not be undone

His manly stamen, now tumescent,
    Planted seeds inside her unfolding crescent.
First they communed
    Then they swooned.

Together they sang of their moment sublime
    That transcended Space and surpassed Time.
And they gave thanks to God who Gave life
    To Adam, the husband, and Eve, the wife.

Jasmine blossoms perfumed the air
    And nightingales were heard everywhere.
A host of Angels in heaven above
    Sang anthems extolling connubial love.

And every woman, possesses the water,
    Which nurtured Eve, God's first daughter.
And every man to this very day
    Carries within him Adam's DNA.

THE FIRST DAWN

Slowly slats of sunshine broke through the dark
    And songs of morning sprung from the meadow lark.

Eve gazed at Adam; Adam stared at Eve
    And together they said, "For the Blessings we receive

Thank You, God." And at dawn they were renewed
    And from each there did exude
Ribbons of bounty from Heaven above
    Sent to Earth from God with Love.

And the two found it fitting to begin each day
    Thanking God in the very same way.
And this legacy they bequeathed to all:
    Listen with your heart to God's Loving Call:

"Make this world a better place
    And crown it with the glory of My Holy Grace."
And so each day they improved Creation
    And each night they sang songs to God with adoration.

ADAM'S FEAR OF THE DARK

Adam watched the white sleek frames of crowds of egrets drifting in
    the twilight sky,
    Ribbons of dappled crimson were turning gray.
A fear seized Adam that he was losing his sight he had not known the
    night before.
    His heart beat faster than a fly's wings; his hands were wet as rain.

In a panic he summoned The Maker.
    After having seen Your magnificent Creation, am I forever to be in
    darkness?
Will I ever again see azure clouds? trees stretching their arms? birds in
    flight?
    Will I ever again see mountain peaks? the turquoise blue of rolling
    rivers?

Will I forever be without light? Adam asked.
    "Worry not," God Calmed Adam, the darkness was made for sleep.
"Most living creatures sleep in the darkness then awake in the light.
    It is their rhythm. Lions, sheep, elephants, crows have it among
    My Creatures.

This is your time, Adam, to sleep, to renew yourself.
    Yours has been a busy day naming and cataloging all of the plants
    and animals."
Adam prepared piles of thatch: one for him and one for Eve.
    They laid their heads upon them.

Their eyes stared at the silver crescent glowing in the sky
    And scanned the sprays of twinkling stars dotting the dark night.
As he listened to the coo-cooing of the owl,
    And the wolves playful howl and the sonar pulses of bats on the
    prowl,

About to ask God why in the dark they must sleep
    Angels into his eyes slumber did sweep.

LOSS OF PARADISE: VERSION ONE

In the beginning of Time, it was thought, that the serpent was the slyest of creatures of the field. He said unto Eve, "even though God said that you should not eat of any tree in The Garden. taste it anyway. It is a delight." The woman replied, "of the fruit of the trees of The Garden we may eat but not of the tree in the midst of The Garden." And the serpent said you will not surely die. God Will Not Know that you have eaten thereof. Your eyes will be opened and you will know good and evil." The woman saw that the tree was a delight to the eyes and its fruit would make her wise. She ate and gave a taste to her husband. Then they heard the Voice of God. Gen III, 1-8.

The sly serpent, it is said,
    Planted an idea in Woman's head,
To eat of the fruit of the Tree
    That would make her wise and make her free.
But instead of gaining wisdom
    She and Adam lost their freedom
And would forever pay the price
    Of their trespass in Paradise:
Both saw they were without any clothes
    And shame colored their faces as red as rose.

LOSS OF PARADISE: VERSION TWO

Adam asked, "Eve where are you hiding? I'll find you."
    A tortoise lumbered toward him and he climbed on its back.
They wandered hither and yon seeking Eve.
    As the sun was setting over the azure sea,
The skies were turning orange and pink.
    Then a red cloud passed by and opened its windows
Raining iridescent, beads of pearls.
    Yellow finches swarmed about to catch them.
The beads dropped to the ground and grew into tall trees with spindly
    branches.
    On each branch was a savory golden fruit.
Eve! There you are! Come out of hiding. Do not pick the fruit!
    She ate. It was sweet! Its nectar burst in her mouth!

"Let me taste it," he begged. "What ecstasy!!!
    O God! What have I done? My hands tremble.
        My legs are frozen. My loins scream.
My arms are heavy with sleep. My soul is slipping away.
    I am no longer Adam. I am Man. I am naked. So are you."
Eve answered, "I lusted after the fruit but did not taste it
    Until the sly serpent urged me to do so.
The serpent told me that he is the deputy of the Creator.
    Whatever is in the garden is ours.
I bit the skin and sweet nectar trickled on to my tongue then down my
    throat.
    My breasts titillated; my eyes sparkled;
My hands trembled; my legs froze.
    I looked at me then looked at you
And we were both naked. I was so ashamed.
    Lightning branches scudded through the blackened skies.
My arms are heavy with sleep and my soul is slipping away.
    I am no longer Eve. I am Woman.
In the morning when we awake
    We will pluck leaves from the umbrella plant and wrap ourselves
        in them."

The two moved toward one another
> Their skins tingled with the touch of the other.

Each bonded to the other in sensuality, joy, and shame
> Then lapsed into fitful sleep.

When the sun melted the night,
> Adam awoke. Eve was no longer next to him.

He called to her.
> His voice trilled like a flute echoing throughout the valley.
> "Where is your hiding place ? Are you behind a rock?

Come out. Let's gambol by the stream
> Let's stand beneath the waterfall and wash away the heat of the morning."

"My hands will comb your silken tresses.
> My lips will taste them; my nose will sip your delicate fragrance.

Your gazelle pines for you.
> The zephyr rises and will cool your breasts.

Let us again drink of the sweet nectar of the peaches."

Adam was no longer in a familiar place.
> Eden was a dream that evaporated.

Eve stepped out of the woods clothed in the leaves of the umbrella plant.
> She handed Adam a leaf to conceal his loins.

Hand in hand they walked away from the Valley of Yesterday.
> God's Angry Words etched in their brains followed them throughout the day.

"You disobeyed My commandment.
> Enmity will divide you from others.
> With ebbing strength you will sow your seed and reap your harvest.

With the sweat of your brows will you eat your bread.
> Your sorrows will multiply.
> Never forget your disobedience and err never again.

Teach your children to obey My Words and their children will learn from their example.
>> You and your children will know no rest until, lifeless, you rejoin the dust of Earth

From whence you sprang.
>> From dust you came and to dust will you return.
> You are blessed and you are cursed.

The bridge between us is broken.
> You and all of your descendants will spend their lives repairing it.
>> I Am God. "

THE ASP'S LAMENT

The lowly asp slith'rd slowly down
    The Tree of Life in Eden's Wood.
Slinking through the rock-strewn path,
    Adam, First Man, of flesh and mind,
Of earth and sea, of joy and tears
    Was teaching beasts God's Moral Laws
Which he himself never fully understood,
    Or without hope of reward,
Entirely practiced. Thou shalts; thou musts;
    Do not; must not. But he and Eve
God's Commandment ignored and breached
    And with cunning projected blame
On guileless me. I, first victim,
    In history accuse you Man
Of duplicity. The tale you altered
    So you would look pure. You called me "snake"
In derision. What's done is done!
    I forgive you. Before losing
My power of speech, to you I say,
    Admit the truth 'though it may sting.
Could I, an innocent asp, with a brain inferior
    Persuade you, man, with the brain superior
To disobey God's Commandment?
    For acts of your own design
        You, alone, are responsible. Amen! Amen!

LILITH, QUEEN OF THE NIGHT[2]

Lilith, Queen of the Night, slyly slithers into the human heart
    And germinates seeds of passion
Sown by the Creator at the beginning of Time.
    In a cosmic burst she opens the gates of carnal pleasure
And steals the blues, greens, and reds
    Hiding within a black curtain,
Separating fleeing Apollo from Saturn's grasp,
    And mixes them as they coalesce
Into an epiphany of angles, lines and arching curves.
    Percolating lightning, she twists tongues of orange flame
And flings them at Man and his Woman
    Who helplessly writhe in pleasure
Enchanted, deceived, and destroyed.
      She taunts us from the deepest recesses of our brains.
        We must resist.

---

2. *Lilith, a winged demonic spirit in Semitic legends flies about at night with thousands of pernicious Angels. For many ages Jewish women wore amulets to protect their families from her. One legend depicts her as Adam's first wife from whom monsters issued. She sought equality with him. Rejected, she flew off into the night speaking God's Ineffable Name. She is referred to as a spirit who lays waste the land for centuries. Isa XXXIV:14.*

THE FIRST FAMILY: VERSION ONE

And the man experienced Eve, his wife; and she became pregnant and gave birth to Cain,[3] and said, "I have become a mother with the help of God. And once again became pregnant and gave birth to Abel, Cain's brother. Gen IV, 1.

Adam and Eve under one another's spell
    Dissolved in passions neither could quell.
They coupled when the sun was bright
    And coupled, too, while watching stars at night

Then within Eve's most mystic place
    A creature grew from only a trace
Of life. Her monthly blood stopped its flow
    And she felt a heaviness down below.

Her pelvis was strong enough to withstand strain
    As well as the movements of the unborn Cain.
But many a morning she'd wake up queasy
    Whatever was happening was not easy

On her digestion. She began to worry
    That Adam might catch it in a hurry-
The problem that within her was brewing.
    So she asked him to stop what he was doing

And to pray to God for information
    Or, perhaps, some confirmation
That whatever it was she was undergoing
    Was within her realm of knowing.

She should, after all, understand her state
    Given that she forbidden fruit once ate,

---

3. *May either be derived from the Hebrew "kanah" to purchase or "kayn" a nest.*

The one that on her bestowed intuition
    Should have explained her indisposition

And her weight gain—but did not.
    Adam prayed. God Answered the fact you have sought
Is this: within Eve a creature is growing
    From the ecstasy you both were knowing.

One instant when fathoming her you did together conceive
    A new life: one part Adam and one part Eve.
What features that creature will possess
    I must confess.

I Cannot Predict because when sperm and ovum do their dance
    What happens next is due to chance.
Eve will feel heavy, her breasts will swell,
    And there are a few more things I must tell

You. Like a melon round will she be
    And she'll feel a strain about each knee.
This will make her walk like a duck.
    But that is truly a stroke of luck

Because it means the child inside
    Is growing long as Eve is growing wide.
Yet she will feel beautiful, just like a queen,
    The first human mother that has ever been.

Eve sparkled with a rosy glow
    As her hand guided his to show
What they both had done
    One moment under a palm tree shading the sun.

There was much to do to build a nest
    And furnish it with the very best.
Trees to be cut and stones to be hewn.
    Together they built a safe cocoon.

Then one day Eve felt an urgent strain;
    There were tears of joy mixed with stabs of pain.
Dear husband she said drawing near is the time
    For us to witness a moment sublime.

Rotating slowly, without making a sound,
    The being in her womb turned upside down.
A head first pushed its way towards the light
    And was sliding from her canal with all its might.

Eve pushed and puffed in the heat of the day
    And a round hairy head inched its way
From between her legs. It's a pear with hair
    Adam said of him who was to become his son and heir.

But Eve was dizzy with sweat and pain
    From the arduous effort as well as the strain
Of giving birth. Her mind conjured images of the garden fruit,
    The seductive serpent, the eviction, and the route

Out of Eden. But the memories were jumbled.
    The images were clotted and Eve's lips mumbled
Thoughts which were spinning, spinning, spinning
    In her brain like a circle without end, without beginning.

When it seemed that her energy was spent
    She touched Adam's face who over her was bent.
Suddenly there was an urgent rush
    And the child oozed out in a reddish gush.

Eve shouted Thank you God!
    With a palm frond Adam sawed
The cord that connected mother with child.
    He knotted the cord and smiled.

Then he stroked the child's back. It expelled
>   Mucous that within its mouth had welled.
It breathed a hardy cry
>   Resounding as it spiraled toward the sky.

Adam mopped the brow of Eve, his love,
>   With a patch of wool Sent from God Above.
He washed the child and wrapped him in a leaf.
>   Amazed beyond belief,
It's a miracle, he said to Eve
>   For us to receive
A child who is one part yours and one part mine
>   Sent to us by God Divine.

They held each other's hands to pray
>   To God for the blessing they received that day.
Thank you God for the gift of life
>   That grows from the love of husband and wife.

Eve cradled the babe in her soft, warm arms
>   And sang to him with all of her charms,
"May peace and goodness into your being flow,"
>   And the voice of God Whispered, "Let it be so."

THE FIRST FAMILY: VERSION TWO

And it came to pass, when the number of humans expanded and daughters were born unto them, that the sons of God saw that the daughters of men were appealing and they took them as wives. God Saw the wickedness of mortals was great and every idea they had was evil. Gen VI, 1–2, 5.

The Garden of Eden where two humans dwelled,
    Was filled with sweet ambrosia they daily smelled,
What a time of grand delight,
    Filling cups with joy by day and night.

The Creator Said," Obey My laws
    Stray not for any cause."
But the humans tested the Divine Command,
    And were sent away from the exotic land.

Together the humans worked the stubborn soil;
    Blistered hands, reward for toil.
And when the land blossomed into flower,
    They gave thanks to God's All Mighty Power.

Adam and Eve loved each other.
    First came Cain and then Abel, his brother.
Each brother planned his own survival
    And soon became the other's rival.
Cain farmed the land; Abel tended sheep.
    Abel carded wool and Cain had grain to reap.
Each sought to be the one to be pleasing to God
    And to be the only one God Would Laud.

One day in a fit of rage,
    Which he could not curb or at all assuage,
Cain struck Abel upon the head.
    Abel fell down and lay there dead.

God Wept for Abel, a righteous son,
    And Scolded Cain for what he had done.
Cain heard the words, "It is wrong to smite
    Whether one is wrong or another is right."

But God Wept for Cain, a faithful son, too.
    Whose act of murder he would always rue.
Sorrow to both at that moment were wed
    But would never bring back Abel who lay there dead.

Cain then wandered from land to land
    To find relief for his reprimand.
There were no words that would him console;
    There was no mercy for his sullied soul.

Adam and Eve, filled with grief,
    Grieved for their sons without relief.
Their sadness cast deep a spell forlorn,
    Until to them another son was born.

Seth, their son, became heir to the land
    Beyond the horizons his eyes had scanned.
In turn, he willed it to the-yet-to-be-born
    The jewels who would God's Crown adorn.

ENDLESS EMPTY ECHOES OF MURDER

When Cain and Abel were in the field, Cain rose up against his brother and murdered him. Gen IV, 8. The story is said to be based on the Sumerian legend of Inanna, chief goddess, which represent the conflict between farmers and ranchers. Dumuzi, belligerent god of the shepherds, competes for her attention with Enkimdu. the easy going god of the farmers. Enkimdu tells Dumuzi to marry Inanna and then wanders away. In another version of the legend Inanna has Dumuzi murdered.

The thematic similarities of the Sumerian and the Hebrew legends are inescapable. Themes of belligerence, placidity, and murder are present in both stories although Abel, the shepherd, is the pacific one and Cain wanders away. At another level this is an allegory of good and evil found in some form in many cultures.

According to the Qu'ran urged on by a raven Cain buried Abel. Cain regretted his action. [al-Ma'idah: 27–31], In the Gospel according to Matt XXV, 35 Abel, the first martyr, is regarded as righteous. He is also mentioned in the Canon of the Mass.

A tear dropped a million years ago from a mother's eye
    And fell into the sea of grief where mothers go to cry.
Eve, urmother of us all, having borne two sons in woe
    Fed them from her milky breasts from which mother love did
        flow.

She taught them to accept God who Created everything
    And from their abundant bounty a thanks offering to bring.
Abel offered fattened sheep; Cain, scraps of the field.
    When God Favored Abel's gift, a rage in Cain reeled.

Cain grabbed a pointed rock and crushed his brother's skull.
    Abel slumped to the ground- bloodied, lifeless, null.
Eve's eyes filled up with tears, bitterly she cried.
    He who swam inside her womb lay lifeless by her side.

Her fingers touched the bleeding wound, then caressed the breasts that fed
    The innocent shepherd, Abel, now prostrate before her dead.
Cain reached out to touch her hand but, heartsick, she turned away in pain
    And staggered to be free of him who had his brother slain.

Cain raised the rigid corpse onto his sweating back.
    And blood droplets dripped from the skull that sustained the crack.
He walked in sun, he walked in rain; no shelter did he find
    A heavy heap of Abel lay on his shoulder and on his mind.

Cain wandered east of Eden, his sorrowing shoulders sagged
    With his rigid brother Abel, a burden to be dragged.
Cain shrieked, "Forgive me "every night in terror-dreams.
    But Abel made no sound at all 'though Cain heard explosive screams.

Weary worn at dawn he'd 'wake and traveled by the light,
    And fought off attacking vultures until dusk met the waiting night.
The stench of Abel filled the air, no longer could Cain a morsel eat.
    He felt his strength was ebbing and a swelling in his feet.

His back was bent and drooping low when his feet toyed with the sea
    And as he stepped into a wave Abel slipped off quietly.
Cain was not aware that Abel had dropped into the deep,
    His shoulders sensing a heavy load causing him to creep.

He crawled along the edge of Time although the light was dim
    And saw his mother Eve and toward her began to swim.
"Mama, mama, comfort me ! "I'm dying for what I've done."
    Cain pleaded with Eve losing another son.

But Eve trembled and turned away, her body in a chill.
    There was no mercy for a son who would his brother kill.
Cain's keening filled her ears and ever lingered there;

On her face were bitter tears; in her soul was deep despair.

> For one full year did she mourn;
> Then a third son to her was born.
> Torrents of joy purged her grief
> That had stolen her bliss like a thief.

THE BEGINNING OF EVIL

When families on earth became more abundant, divine creatures noticed the beauty of the daughters and married them. Gen. VI, 1

When the sons of the heavenly creatures
    Looked upon the daughters of mortals
Their hearts pounded with delight
    And their knees melted from passion.
They took these daughters as their wives
    And from their offspring proceeded evil
But also Forces of good from the Mind of God
    Which was the template of mortals.
And forever would evil and good contend.

FRUIT OF THE WOMB

From the seeds of passion's flow'r buds of joy unfold and smile at the world about.
    The fruit of the womb ripens exuding beauty unparalleled in the past.

EVE MUSES AT ADAM'S DECLINE

Eve bent over Adam and lovingly drew his eyelids closed, her own eyes
    wet with grief.
    She drifted into nostalgia. How many tides, she mused,
Has the moon pulled in its journey through our lives.
    How many sunrises have there been to bring on the day;
How many sunsets brought on the night. Time deserts us.
    Brushing wisps of his sparse silver hair, she spoke to Adam, his face
        blue with death,
        These past few months have been especially hard for you,
    Your manhood was stolen; your incontinence, embarrassing; your
        nausea, constant.
        The little you ate came back.
           Remember how tenderly I washed your face
And changed your clothes? Your cough still echoes in my ears.
    I hear each rasp. Then fright returns to me.
Staring at me blankly, you seemed to be asking, "Who am I ?
    Where am I?
    How did I get this way? What will happen next?"

The man I admired has shriveled. Your mind was confused,
    Filled with forgetting yet recalling what never happened.
You blamed God for Entrapping us to sin in the garden.
    You thought that Seth murdered Abel
And that it was he who wandered East of Eden.
    When he came to visit, you called him Cain.
We both knew that meaning had drifted out of your life.
    You were languishing in a river of forgetfulness and drowning in a
        sea of anguish.
I wish I had eaten from the Tree of Life instead of from the Tree of
    Knowledge.
    Maybe you would still be with me.
        But once done an act cannot be annulled!
        Can anyone reverse History?
To cheer you, I told you stories about your kindness, your virility, your
    passion.
    You smiled an empty smile.

How roused you were to pity when a frail horse had fallen along the wayside.
> How your hands lovingly caressed my face, my arms, my breasts.

I swoon thinking about how beautiful it had been to make babies with you.
> I felt young again. You nodded blankly. Did you understand the words of my heart?

How tender you had been to the infant Cain and later to the baby Abel.
> Both drank of my milky breasts. I tingled with joy as they nursed at my teats.

You held each babe in your arms; in a voice like the nightingale you sang hymns to God.
> How, frightened yourself, you confronted the wild cat poised to menace our babies.

When they grew up you taught them so much:
> How to sow, how to reap, how to tend sheep, how to build, and, above all, how to pray.

How pained you were when Cain took Abel's life away. You said nothing. You were wooden.
> Can any difference between Children of God be so chafing as to justify murder?

We lost a child. What did Cain gain?
> Marked by God, he wandered in fear, in guilt, and in grief.

You hurt, too, but you wanted to be with him to soften his pain.
> They were such dear children. Heartaches they gave us, though.

They were a crucible mixing jealousy, strife, rage, and, above all, love.
> Seth made up for the two of them. We could count on him to make us smile.

The jokes he would tell about the tiger and the leopard.
> And he made us feel proud, too. So gentle, so methodical, so wise.

Abel never left your mind, though.
> You must have been sensing your oncoming death,

Hugging a dead donkey lying along the path and calling it Abel.
> Your eyes clouded up and droplets of tears fell to the ground.

I, too, had a foreboding,
> But I did not know when would be your last breath.

God Keeps us guessing, or, perhaps, Has us cling to a thin thread of hope

That we still can be of use tomorrow.
> We are to make every moment count.

And how useful you had once been!
> Your hands were not always so calloused.

In Eden they had been as smooth as rose petals.

After we were evicted, they became rough making axes
> And calloused felling trees, stripping bark, building a home.

How arduous it was to break clods of earth, muddy from the seasonal rains.
> But you did all those things.

By the sweat of your brow did you plant and reap grain.
> By the sweat of your brow did we eat bread.

Then there were sheep to shear and clothes to sew.
> How cleverly you planned for the cold and the drought.

You did all things without complaint and with no thought of receiving praise.
> Praise God, you would say. Thank God, you would proclaim.

It was for the family's welfare that you labored.
> Then you were chilled.
>> When you trembled I warmed you with an elephant leaf;

Then you trembled and I rubbed your arms with lamb's wool.
> Then you lifted submerged feelings sleeping since the loss of our boys

And grew agitated with agony and morose with melancholy.
> Then your brain exploded.
>> Your thoughts scattered hither and thither.

Your mind was chaos.
> Your heart stopped beating and your face turned cold.
> Ours was True Love and I will cherish your memory until stars lose their glitter.

Eve kissed Adam's stone, lifeless lips and sobbed, "good bye my best friend."

OUT OF EVIL COMETH GOOD IN TIME

And it came to pass that Cain left the Sight of God and drifted to the land of the wanderers, east of Eden. And Cain made love to his wife and she became pregnant and bore Enoch. Gen IV, 16–17.

The penitent Cain took a wife who begat Enoch
    Whose son, Irad, cleansed his father's sin and begat Mehujael
Who cleansed his grandfather's sin and begat Methushael
    Who cleansed the world of his great-grandfather's sin and begat
        Lamech, the pure,
Who begat three sons who expanded God's Creation:
    Jabal bred horses and cattle;
        Jubal taught the world to play the harp and flute;
           And Tubal worked bronze and iron.
        From these three grew economics, art, and science.

NOAH, THE HERO

In ancient Greek lore the hero, either a human elevated to the status of the divine or a demoted divine, was revered as a demigod. Often he was perceived as a ghost to be appeased. In contrast the hero in Biblical literature was no demigod nor someone to be feared. Noah is the exemplar of the Biblical hero. He was a man righteous in his generation but fallible. To the ancient Hebrews, heroes were persons of valor. As humans they erred but as heroes they transcended the ordinary.

From the very beginning the humans that God Created had cavorted with truancy. Adam and Eve were disobedient and Cain took his brother's life. Generations to come developed the arts and technology but they also lived by stealth. Jealous of one another the farmers tried to vanquish shepherds. It is apparent that the species God Created could destroy itself. God, according to the Bible, Became so repulsed by humans that Creation was inundated by a flood.

The Flood legend is found in many cultures ranging from the American Indian to the Icelandic and to the Chinese and Japanese. Closest to the Noah tale is the Sumerian. King Ziusudra is forewarned about the impending flood and builds a boat. There is a deluge after which Utu, the son god, appears. Ziusudra is saved and offers sacrifices to Utu. This tale made its way into the famed Epic of Gilgamesh. Although the Noah tale may have borrowed some of the essentials from the Sumerian, the Noah version has a different argument: Noah was spared so that a new and more moral civilization would take root. Noah made a sacrifice, too. God, however, Regretted having Flooded Creation and Decided never to repeat that error. However, even after the flood waters subsided the descendants of Noah did not cleanse their weaknesses to evil. Noah, righteous in his generation, got drunk and had sexual relations with his daughter-in-law. He, too, was fallible. Thus the ending of the Noah story confutes the beginning which says he was righteous in his generation.

NOAH RECEIVES AND GIVES

Noah's father, Lamech, a direct descendant of Adam,
    Sat face to face with his son
As they fished in iridescent waters
    That would later overflow in heavy rains
And related to him the history of the world since Creation
    As his father, the agéd Methuselah, had related to him
And as fathers before him related to their children for generations.
    Each age had added to the history:
Their discoveries, inventions, tools, insights,
    New emerging species of plants and animals,
Ongoing struggles, victories, defeats, hardships, triumphs, joys, grief,
    Songs, stories, designs, crafts, trades,
And the trove of the family legends.
    Noah learned how his forebears scribed speech,
Counted, added, found angle size, and measured time and space.
    The gentle ripples of the water reflected who they had been
And who they would become.
    So it was with Noah who sat at the river bank with his son Shem
After the flood.
    "Look carefully at the arcing rainbow in the sky," Noah urged
        Shem.
"The multihued bow is God's Compact with us mortals.
    Witness its Sublime Splendor;
Behold how the vaulting heavens fills with awe.
    Never again Will God Flood Creation."
What we must do, as God Taught Adam who taught his son, Seth,
    And he to mortals since for all generations,
Is to revere with love the Creator and not worship false gods,
    To respect life and take no one's life,
To respect the sanctity of marriage and to shun incest,
    To respect the property of others and rob no one,
To eat fruits, vegetables, cooked meat and fish but eat no flesh of a living creature,
    To be merciful and judge every human fairly."

And Shem taught these laws and human history to posterity.
> Abram, direct descendant of Adam learned them from Terah, his father,

As they fished on the river banks watching the rippling, iridescent dappled droplets
> Primed in the vaulting Heaven.

And he leaned them well.

NOAH'S TALE: VERSION ONE

"Noah was a faultless man righteous in his generations who walked with God." Gen VI, 9.

"Noah, Noah. Listen to Me."
    Noah felt a strange energy that wouldn't let him be.
He howled a scream. A nightmare, no a dream.
    "Noah, Noah. Listen." Once again he heard a mystic sound
Within his mind and all around.
He left his bed, fearing his senses had fled.
    I AM GOD, the Voice Declared.
        Noah was awed but unprepared.
How can that be
    That God would be Talking to me?
God Replied,
    I Am always by your side.

Why Talk to me, Noah thought.
    God Said, You are the one I have Sought:
Someone just and fair is hard to find
    Then I Saw that you are gentle and kind.

Noah! Listen! This is what I Have Planned:
    I Am Going to Flood the land
Because the people have defiled my Creation.
    Everywhere I Look is abomination.

This is what I Ask;
    And it is no simple task.
Build an ark strong enough to sail
    In seas of a blustering gale.

Noah obeyed God's Command;
    Before relentless waters filled the land
He gathered creatures two by two
    Those that walked and those that flew.

And they all entered the ark:
> Creatures light; creatures dark.

His family came on board
> As the rains gushed and pored.

After many days the creatures were uneasy
> And more than a few became queasy.

Because the ark was rocking in each swell
> And from the gasses dead fish expel.

Noah kneeled and started to pray,
> He hardly knew words to say.

Then these words left his mind
> They were the only words he could find.

Dear God Show us Mercy this day
> To Forgive is Your Way.

Stop the rain; dry the flood.
> Send a wind to scatter the crud.

A spume of water began to subside
> And here and there the land was dried.

No longer was there a storm
> Instead the sun shone and it was warm.

All beheld a curved beauty bowing above
> Every color Sent by God Above.

Noah took a dove in hand
> And asked it to scout out the land.

Very soon back it flew
> With an olive leaf dipped in dew.

Mrs. Noah raised her voice
> With prayer did she rejoice.

Noah, with his mission ended,
> Saw that the creatures each other had befriended.
And that generation of Creatures found release
> And for many years lived in peace.

NOAH'S TALE: VERSION TWO

When the world was still young in years
    And each land was probed by pioneers,
New plants and creatures were still arising
    In lovely forms, at times, surprising.

Some years the hot sun burned the land
    And dried the rich soil to sparkling sand.
In other years the rains each day
    Would wash the roots of crops away.

During the times with little to eat,
    Life was bitter and rarely sweet.
But instead of working with one another,
    People cheated and robbed each other.

They were greedy and selfish as well,
    Their very own children they would sell.
This is not what God Had in Mind
    When the humans Were first Designed.

Then there arose within God's Plan
    A humble hero, a righteous man.
This modest mortal, Noah, his name,
    Who sought no glory and sought no fame.

God called to Noah, "Listen with care.
    A flood will come. You must prepare."
Noah felt a shiver. His spine was a river of chill
    When called upon to serve Merciful God's Will.

God Had Planned to bring on a flood
    And Bury the sinners in heaps of mud.
At God's Command, Noah built a ship
    And brought provisions for the trip.

All manner of life did he take,
    From land, from sea, and from the lake.
The only mortals who would be saved
    Were Noah and his kin who were not depraved.

Then walls of rain fell in force;
    Noah wondered what was to be his course.
But God Showed Noah what was to be the way
    And Noah went forth without delay.

After many days the spastic waters abated
    As Noah's crew anxiously awaited.
And as the waters purled placidly along
    All on board sang a song

"We thank You God for rains suspending
    Bringing us to our journey's ending.
We pledge to You to repair Creation
    And treat each other with toleration."

After the days of endless rain,
    A brilliant sun dried the muddied terrain.
It is but a mirage said his wife.
    No replied Noah I see signs of life.

A honeyed coo rose from a dove of peace
    And with Noah's caress was given release.
The dove went forth, his journey brief,
    And returned to Noah with an olive leaf.

This was a sign that to all revealed
    That the liquid land had finally healed.
When the ark docked the sky turned blue
    And all left the ark to start life anew.

ABRAM LEAVES HOME AND BECOMES ABRAHAM

God said to Abram, "depart your country, leave your kin, and your father's home and go to a land that I Will Show you. You will have many descendants and they will become a great nation. I will Bless you and you will be well known. Gen, XII, 1–2.

Ur, city of the moon goddess,
    Was no longer a haven to Terah, Abram's father, of Noah's line.
He gathered his family, collected all possessions,
    Crossed the river and trekked to Haran, a new moon away.
They journeyed through the blistering heat of the day.
    Sand storms blinded the eyes,
Heavy rains soaked through the skin, and freezing night cold chilled their bones.
    Haran was an oasis. Merchants gathered there and sold their wares.

Terah grew rich fashioning gods to satisfy all worshiping leanings.
    The people welcomed the newcomers.
The newcomers had arrived with wealth
    And there increased their fortune.

The people trusted them because they were kind and just.
    If anyone was in need, the newcomers, the river crossers, the Habiru, gave freely.
The newcomers, the river crossers, the Habiru, knew ways to settle disputes
    That always split one mortal from another.

Abram was gifted with wisdom and compassion.
    And many sought his counsel.
Abram questioned his father on the divinity of molded clay and shaped wood.
    "How can an inert moon reflect sun light and yet control our destinies?

Could your idols *found* the world?
>Could your idols *create* animals, plants, and mortals?"

"They offer solace, hope, and fertility to their owners,"
>Was his father's reply. Abram did not accept his account.

He had been awe struck by God's Mystic Design.
>He sought to understand the marvelous onset of the cosmos.

Then, deep within him a Soft yet Stalwart Voice Rose and Called
>"Abraham, Abraham!"
>Abram replied. "Here I am."

"Henceforth you are to be called 'Abraham'.
>Because you will become the father of many peoples

I Have Given your name an extra letter to raise your rank.
>That letter, H, is a Part of Me, and is My Gift to you to Crown your name.

Henceforth, Your wife Sarai, will be called Sarah, a princess.
>Then the Voice Instructed him with these words,

"Gather your courage and go forth from your father's house.
>Go hither to the land I Will Show you.

To your offspring will I Give this land."
>Abraham, clad in God's Everlasting Love,

Bade farewell to his father.
>He took his possessions, his dear wife and princess Sarah, and his nephew Lot

And followed A Spark of Divine Light, his Compass,
>From one land to another, until he stopped at Canaan, home of the Hittites.

There the Divine Voice Spoke,
>"To your offspring I Give this land. Be fruitful and multiply!"

At that place Abraham built an altar dedicated to the Glinting Light
>Which he knew to be from God.

But his wife, his beloved, his princess, his Sarah, was barren.

She was without child.

Abraham spoke to "God" and asked how can he have offspring with a barren wife.

"Be patient, Abraham!" God Urged him.

And Abraham told Sarah of his conversation with "God."

She guffawed.

"How can I an old woman, nearly ninety, become a mother?"

Abraham searched his mind to find answers but they were beyond his knowing.

In the meantime he took Hagar, Sarah's maid servant, and she bore him a son.

In time a swollen bud of love enlarged within Sarah

Into a curve, splendid like the rainbow that Noah witnessed after the Flood.

In time the bud of love had its own existence and was named "Isaac,"

To remind her that once she laughed at God. And now God Laughed back.

SARAH, THE MATRIARCH

And the Egyptians beheld the Sarah and admired her beauty. Gen XII, 14

Her countenance was comely
    Her mind was razor honed
And the fiber of her spirit,
    With Mercy had been Toned.

Daily would she talk with God
    Who Listened to every phrase
And Heard the language of her heart
    And Praised her gentle ways.
One day Sarah heard A Call
    As if in Mystic Dream,
Leave Haran with your man
    And follow My Sacred Beam.

Abraham heeded his wife's advice
    And left Haran for good
And traveled toward an unknown land,
    Hopeful of fatherhood.

Sarah arranged the journey
    She knew what was the way
Because God Had Showed her in her Dream
    The road so's not to stray.

In every land where she set foot
    The people extolled her brain
And she would greet them regally
    With a simple refrain,

God Is in every heart
    To Make Humanity pure
And Crown Creation with decency
    And every ill to Cure.

Sarah showed the world that beauty
    Is not a flawless face,
Not ruby lips nor henna hair,
    But Kindness born of Grace.

She taught the world
    That majesty is everyone's right and claim;
All it takes is valor
    And a noble aim.

THE FATE OF SODOM

God Said, "loudly wail the Sodomites for galling are their sins." Gen XVIII, 20.

The people of Sodom, renowned for guile
    Attacked every stranger in ways quite vile.
They robbed, they knifed, and set homes on fire
    And against their own kind would often conspire.

"They've scorched my land," God Tearfully Spoke,
    "And defiled what is sacred just as a joke."
God Urged them to treat Creation with kindness sincere,
    But they just jabbed at strangers and provoked intense fear.

God's Commandments the Sodomites ignored,
    No matter the Mercy with which they were Implored.
God Judged it best Sodom to Raze.
    To rid the world of its hurtful ways.

Was such a verdict just and right?
    God Dispatched Heralds to Sodom before the fall of night.
They stayed with Lot, Abraham's kin,
    Who, though better than most, was not without sin.

They Sought proof that Sodom should be saved.
    But what They found, instead, was a community depraved.
The saddened Envoys Found no reason to believe
    That the people of Sodom deserved a Reprieve.

In fact the people of Sodom set out snares
    Against anyone whose ways were different from theirs.
They banged at Lot's door to kill the Envoys God Sent,
    But Lot drove them away to thwart their ill intent.

With heavy heart, God Decided the fate
    Of the city of evil and exporter of hate.
God Thought the matter over. It was carefully reviewed.
    Then Told Abraham how Sodom would be Subdued.

"Abraham," Reported God, "Sodom will burn.
    I must be Just but I must also be Stern.
Let all peoples learn that God Despairs
    Of those who harm others of ways differ from theirs."

Abraham knew Sodom was a blight on the land
    But destruction would reduce Sodom city to mere sand.
Why raze a city and kill both the good and the bad
    Abraham asked himself in a mood that was sad .

Humbly Abraham asked if God really would Waste
    Those who are guilty as well as those who are chaste?
He asked God if, perhaps, fifty righteous were found,
    Would Sodom still be burned down to the ground?

God Replied, "if fifty righteous were found,
    Sodom would not burn to the ground."
"Were the number of righteous but forty-five,"
    Abraham asked modestly, "would they remain alive"?

God Replied that if the number of righteous were but forty-five,
    Sodom would be saved and that city would thrive.
"But what if the number equals the fingers on each hand,"
    Bargained Abraham meekly, "Would You, then, let Sodom stand?"

God Replied if the righteous of Sodom numbered but ten,
    Spared would be Sodom's women and men.
But only self righteous were found in the city,
    And a stony fire consumed Sodom without any pity.

ISAAC AT THE MOUND: VERSION ONE

And God tested Abraham and called, "Abraham" who answered "Here I am." Take now your son, your beloved son, your, Isaac, and go to the land of Moriah and offer him as a sacrifice upon the mountain I will show you." Gen XXII, 1–2.

God Searched the world for a flawless soul
    To shape in history the patriarch's role:
Teacher to every generation
    And an ideal of goodness to every nation.

Such a man must obey
    God's Commands without delay.
To Judge if Abraham was that very one,
    God Asked him to give up Isaac, his son.

"My Isaac? my dearest one?"
    "If he is gone, I'll lose Sarah's son."
Thus Abraham questioned The Voice.
    But he heard the Wind Whisper, "he is My choice."

Up the mountain the two then trod,
    According to directions Given by God.
Isaac saw wood for the fire
    But no lamb that offerings would require.

"God will Provide," Abraham told his son,
    As fires for the off'ring had already begun.
Then Abraham bound Isaac to the altar site
    And unsheathed his knife, glinting with light.

"Abraham, Abraham" A Voice Called from Above,
    A Sobbing Voice Filled with Merciful Love,
"Hurt not the boy; cause him no harm!"
    And in midair Was Stopped Abraham's arm.

Abraham wept copious tears
    On that day and for the rest of his years
And so did God whose cruel request
    Was a lesson to the world, not just a test.

ISAAC AT THE MOUND: VERSION TWO

What son who had already reached the age of knowing
    Would climb the dusty, sacred mound with his father
As he sensed from the firestone and knife in his father's hand
    And the wood he carried for the sacrificial fire that there was no lamb for the sacrifice?

A trusting one.

What father who waited until he was 100 years old to realize his seed,
    Climbed the dusty, sacred mound with his son, the only child of his beloved Sarah,
And with palms wet with sweat held firmly to the firestone
    And to the unsheathed knife gleaming in the hot sun while the son
Carried the wood, both knowing there was no lamb for the sacrifice?

An obedient one.

What God would Ask of Abraham to give up his son, the first Hebrew circumcised
    At eight days, risking extinction of the line at the dusty, sacred mound,
As the father seized the firestone and the unsheathed knife scintillating in the hot sun
    While the son carried the wood, all three knowing there was no sacrificial lamb?

A Trusting One.

Then a shaft of Light born of the God of Love
    Melted the darkness that spread in the Heavens above.
        The forgiveness in God's Breast
            Commanded Abraham, "cease its my behest."

What God, then, wet with tears and Regretting the assignment to the
>	first patriarch,
>	Caused Abraham's hand to stop midair at the dusty, sacred mound
So it touched not Isaac, the patriarch to be, on the altar of the dusty,
>	sacred mound?

>	*A Contrite One.*

ABIMELECH TEACHES ABRAHAM A LESSON

Abraham informed Abimelech, the king, that Sarah was his sister. The king took Sarah into his palace. God then Appeared to the king in a dream and Told him that he would die because he had taken a woman who is already married. Abimelech did not approach her again. Gen, XX 1 ff,

From his palace window high above the town
    Abimelech gazed at Sarah in her billowing gown.
What an alluring figure; what a comely face
    What regal carriage; what style; what grace.

        He hungered for her, so pretty and so fair
           To sire through her womanhood a royal heir.
        But the royal bed was filled with woe,
           His stream of semen refused to flow.

An eerie dream filled his aching head;
    Stricken with fear, he lay like stone in his bed
Because the Hebrew God, in ghostly disguise,
    Unmasked Abraham and his lies.
        Not a sister was Sarah but his wife-
           He had practiced deceit to save his own life.

    Abraham! Abraham! Listen to this "goy"[4]
        I was led astray by your cowardly ploy.
    Have the courage to speak the truth
        Less than that would be uncouth.

---

4. Gentile.

SARAH'S DEATH

And Sarah said to Abraham cast out the woman, Hagar, for her son must not be your heir with Isaac. And the matter afflicted Abraham on account of his son. Gen XXI, 10-11.

And Sarah was 127 years old when she died in Kiryat Arbah which is Hebron in the land of Canaan and Abraham came to grieve mourning his Sarah. Gen XXIII, 1-2.

As Abraham raised his hand holding the scintillating knife,
    A mob of ravens circled Abraham about to take Isaac's life.
Anticipating the kill they swooped down on the youth
    And sped away to tell Sarah the truth.
Three baby ravens remained watching from a tree
    And saw the knife stop according to God's Decree.
But the congress of ravens winged their way to Sarah, Abraham's wife,
    With the news that Abraham had taken Isaac's life.

Sarah, distraught at the news, heard a lambkin bleating.
    That's my Isaac and her heart stopped beating.
The ravens arrived the news to update
    But Sarah had died; their news was too late.

HAGAR AND SARAH

A hoarse voice despondently wailed,"Hagar! Hagar!"
    No sound was heard but for the silence of passing Time. "Hagar! Hagar!"
No sound was heard but for the peace of those in eternal rest "Hagar! Hagar!"
    No sound was heard but for the echoes of quiet despair. "Hagar! Hagar!
I have searched for you for thousands of years
    In the caves of Judea; in the deserts of Arabia; in the wildernesses of Africa.
How well I understand your hurt, your anger, your vengeance.
    History, too, has hurt me, angered me, made me vengeful.
I look in the mirror and see your woe-stricken face, ashen and punctured, a home to worms.
    My soul anguishes because I have brought you such pain.
I was selfish to want Abraham's seed to be inside of me only
    To be heir to the land. I was cruel to ask Abraham to send you and Ishmael away
To live in the sandy wilds. Let your heart hear my sorrow. I hurt you. I sinned.
    I swim in a sea of contrition. History gnaws at me. I repent. Forgive me.
The mirror shows that we are twin sisters. You, too, are a princess."
The winds that tore the two souls to shreds
    Encircled the decaying ghostly remains
And united Hagar deaf with rage
    To Sarah grieving with guilt.
Each Sister, an urmother,
    Forgave the other
        And became One.

ABIMELECH TEACHES ISAAC A LESSON

Isaac dwelled in Gerar. When asked about Rebecca, fearing for his life, said Rebecca was his sister. One day Abimelech saw Isaac and Rebecca delighting in each other. He reproached Isaac Why did you tell me, the king, that Rebecca is your sister? One of my men might have slept with her and you would be responsible for our guilt. Gen XXVI, 8 ff.

One day when Abimelech was old
    He was watching Rebecca as she strolled.
What an alluring figure; what a comely face
    What regal carriage; what style; what grace.

His loins for her young body did pine
    To renew his youth and enrich his line.
But Isaac called her "sister," though she was his wife,
    Lying like his father to save his life.

Isaac! Isaac! This Philistine goy,
    Is more honest than Abraham or his boy.
Isaac you learned not what you aught
    I will teach again what to your father I taught.
Taint not the truth. Speak no lie
    But paths of virtue beautify.

A FATHER'S BLESSING

When Isaac was old and his eyes were dim he called to Esau and said, I am old, I know not when I will die. Go out to the field and get me a venison and prepare me a tasteful meal that I love and I will give you my blessing." Gen. XXVII, 1–4.

A dusky curtain dropped inside Isaac's eyes.
    Only shadows of memory could he see:
The glitter on his father's knife;
    The sheen on the face of Rebecca, his wife.
And his soul was filled with anguish.
    His remaining days were few.
Who will care for Rebecca, so fine?
    Who will continue my father's line?

There was Esau who hunts,
    Liable to be mauled by his prey
And Jacob who the sheep tends
    Yet on his mother depends.

But my first born Esau, by right,
    Should inherit the land.
Yet Jacob, so refined,
    Was more toward home inclined.

Isaac, perplexed, spoke to God
    Who Illumined his soul.
God replied, "Isaac. It has already been decided.
    Worry not. Rebecca will be well provided.

Since blindness descended upon him
    Isaac's sense of smell had grown keener.
One day he noticed the aroma of a stew
    And a gnawing hunger within him grew.

Who is preparing the mutton?
    "It is I, Esau, father," a shammed gruff voice said.
His hearing had also grown more acute
    And the "I, Esau" he wanted to refute.

"Come closer," Isaac urged.
    And the figure of Jacob drew near.
Isaac stroked the youth's new beard
    To which pieces of camel hair had adhered.

"Coarse like Esau's," Isaac mused.
    And then he inhaled Jacob's clothes
Which had been rolled on the forest floor.
    That forest smell he had known before.

"Esau, my son," Isaac asked
    "Let me taste of your mutton stew."
Jacob gave him a spoon to lick
    And Isaac found the sauce thick

Just like Esau always prepared.
    Then Isaac placed his hands upon Jacob's head.
"Bless you my son, my heir."
    And no longer did Isaac feel despair.

He had fulfilled his paternal duty;
    He blessed his son as Abraham had blessed him.
But guilt shot through Jacob's soul
    It was his brother's birthright that he stole.

He quivered, he shivered.
    He stuttered, he muttered.
His own father he had deceived;
    His own father his lies believed.

Energy filled his legs.
    "G-G-Good bye father, I must leave."
Away he ran, his innocence slain,
    And on his soul a bright red stain.

"Rebecca! Rebecca!" Isaac hoarsely whispered,
    "Give Jacob some gold for his journey."
Isaac had known from the tremor in the voice
    That Jacob was the son who was God's Choice

ISAAC'S PLACE IN HISTORY

God! Isaac humbly spoke to God moments before he died
    Somewhat awed; tongue tied.
I assured You of my faith and constancy at the dusty, sacred mound.
    Why is it that I, the first of Your eternal line,
Alone among the patriarchs with no concubines;
    Did I not make peace with the Philistines who plugged my father's wells?
Why has so little told about me in Your Holy Writ?
    Am I merely a chasm separating my father and my own seed?

At that moment bushes glowed with the Spirit of the Lord
    Zephyrs whispered the Divine Words;
Birds grew silent; lions stifled their roars.
    The universe was still;
        torrents of clouds had halted their rolling paths.

Then Isaac heard God's Answer,
    "You are the dawn that brings on the day light, the dusk that brings darkness at night,
The spark that ignites the fire, the idea that precedes the tool,
    The nerve prod that moves the muscles.
Not a chasm are you Isaac but the bridge across Time
    Connecting your father Abraham and the covenant with posterity.
Judge not the importance of souls by how much is written about them
    But how their existence changed history. "God's Word Was Heard throughout Creation.

JACOB'S MYSTERIOUS DREAM

And (Jacob) dreamed and saw a ladder reaching to Heaven and beheld Angels climbing up and climbing down. And God Stood beside him and Said, "I am the God of Abraham, the God of Isaac. The land upon which you are lying Will I Give to your descendants." Gen XXVIII, 12–14

Rebecca sent Jacob to her older brother.
    Tell Laban, she said, that you were sent by your mother
He will provide you with shelter and with food
    But never forget Jacob, he's wily and shrewd.

Jacob trekked eastward in the dark of the night
    So that Esau would not chase him while he was in flight.
The night was dark, velvet and deep;
    The stars winked at him as he slipped into sleep.

A rock for a pillow,
    The moon aglow;
Jacob's brain recast
    Times that had passed.

He recalled what he to Isaac had said,
    "Father languish not with fever there in your bed.
I vow to will carry on grandfather's line;
    And my children like stars will sparkle and shine.

"Eat of the savories that I, Esau, prepared."
    Jacob's heart then was thumping, his lie still made him scared.
His mind revived his father blessing him there and then,
    It still echoed you are God's Chosen as he blessed him again.

Now asleep he dreamed of a ladder for him to climb
    And he glimpsed into Heaven for a moment sublime.
As he to the top had carefully trod
    He heard from a distance the Sweet Voice of God.

Bless you My Jacob My nation to be
>Extending from desert to the shores of the sea.

When Jacob awoke to continue his trail,
>He blessed the rock and named it Bayt Ayl.[5]

---

5. House of God.

THE CONTRACT WITH LABAN

Jacob loved Rachel and he said to his uncle, Laban, "I will work seven years for my cousin Rachel, your younger daughter. And Laban said I will give her to you rather than another man. Remain with me. Gen XXIX, 18-19.

As Jacob's legs reached Haran, some shepherds he spied.
    "Know ye Laban, my kinsman?" "We do," they replied.
"Approaching with sheep is Rachel, his daughter,
    She comes every day to give her sheep swallows of water."

This woman he dreamed about during his life;
    This is the woman he wanted to be his wife.
Laban gave Jacob shelter and food
    And made him a deal that would include

Seven years of work for his daughter to wed
    As well as her maid to lie in his bed.
He worked his time and was ready Rachel to wed
    But was given as husband to sister, Leah, instead.

Seven more years he labored in the fields of his kin
    And in the end Rachel's heart did he win.
I have another deal said Laban to Jacob one day:
    You want sheep and goats, I'll tell you the way.

Tend my sheep a little while longer
    And I'll give unto you those animals that are the stronger.
Jacob replied, white goats and black sheep are what I will take
    That's the deal with you I will make.

Such goats and sheep are hard to find,
    Agreed to by Laban of treacherous mind.
Then one day Jacob gathered his wives and his sons
    And took Laban's animals, the very best ones.

Laban discovered that he had been cheated;
    At his own game had he been defeated.
Renewed in soul, knowing he was in the right
    Jacob stole away in the dark of night.

P'NAY AYL: THE FACE OF GOD

Jacob was alone when he wrestled with Him Who twisted the hollow of his thigh; and the hollow of his thigh was strained. And He said let Me go for day break is upon us. And Jacob said I will not let You go without Your Blessing. Henceforth, Spoke the Power that Wrenched, your name will be Israel because you have striven (sar) with God (Eyl) and triumphed. And Jacob called the name of the place P'ney-ayl: for I have seen God face to Face and survived. Gen XXXII, 25–31.

A thick curtain of darkness filled the night;
    Only a dim light from a distant star was in sight.
Each night at this time Jacob had been confessing
    The sin he committed to receive Isaac's blessing.

God, he begged, "what will happen to me?
    And what will happen to my progeny?
Esau, fast approaching, is consumed with rage
    Like a wild animal that escaped from his cage.

There will be a grave calamity.
    And my clan and I will only know much misery.
I deserve his hatred. I deceived and cheated.
    It was base of me the way I had Esau treated.

My soul hemorrhages with every tormenting accusation
    And throbs without relief or expiation."
A Figure Approached out of the black.
    "Is that you, Esau, about to attack?"

No voice was heard but he saw Sparkling Eyes
    Scintillating like the stars high in the skies.
The Stranger Grabbed hold of Jacob's thigh,
    A struggle between them did intensify.

They were battling hard when dawn's threads of light
    Cast shadows on the combatants' ardent fight.
"Let Me go," Jacob heard the Cry.
    "If I Don't Return, I Will surely Die."

Jacob knew he had struggled with an Angel Divine
    Who Wanders the Earth until the sun shows its shine.
I will release you when You Bless me,
    Came Jacob's decree.

"You shall be called 'Yis-ra-el,'" the Stranger Replied
    Because with God this night you had vied.
A sacred silence was stilling Time
    And Creation resounded in a moment sublime.

Pulling Jacob's thigh the Stranger Evaporated
    But Jacob's pain never abated.
Beginning then and beyond today,
    As if God's Messenger to repay,

Yisrael limps through history,
    Struggling with God, its nightly destiny.
But when the gates of morn open wide,
    Israel is Blessed and Purified.

JOSEPH AND HIS BROTHERS

And Joseph went after his brothers and found them. And they saw him from afar and before he approached they plotted against him. And they said, "the dreamer draws near. Let us kill him and throw him into a pit and we will say that an evil beast devoured him and we will see then what will happen to his dreams." Gen XXXVII, 17–20.

Rachel, Jacob's lamb, bore Joseph to Jacob's delight.
    Upon this son Shone God's Sacred Light.
Because his brothers were jealous of the favored one,
    They planned to rid Rachel of her only son.

Chaining him, they spat on his face
    And shouted epithets, his soul to debase.
They threw him into a slimy pit, expecting he would die.
    Then a caravan of merchants happened by.

Let's sell to the merchants our worthless half brother,
    Make a small profit and report to his mother
That we were waylaid and Joseph was killed,
    Surely that would be what God Had Willed.

What will you give us for this runaway slave?
    The brothers bartered Joseph and his life did thus save.
Despite the brothers' mean spirit and guile
    Joseph prospered in the land of the Nile.

It came to pass a drought dried Jacob's land,
    There was too little food for his burgeoning band.
So he sent his sons to Egypt to buy grain,
    Enough to last until the next season's rain.

The brothers left with bags of gold,
    They were willing to pay at least sevenfold.
Unknown to them Joseph was Egypt's The Food Commissioner
    And to the needs of all peoples was appointed to administer.

The brothers did not recognize
    Joseph, who was now tall in size.
But Joseph remembered how he had been mistreated
    And how his loving parents had been cheated.

Joseph said I'll sell you grain in return for this young one,
    Pointing to Benjamin, Rachel's other son.
No not that one, they protested, our father's heart will break
    Pick from any of us someone to take.

We've lost one brother and Jacob, our father, nearly died.
    Upon hearing his father's name Joseph cried,
"Judah, Reuben, Gad, Dan and all you others
    Although we're of different mothers

We are kin, I am Joseph whom God Did Save
    From the pit you threw me to be my grave.
The brothers were filled with guilt and flooded with shame
    We are surely to blame

For the misery we've done
    To Jacob, our father, and to you Joseph, his son.
Joseph forgave his brothers the misery they had done
    To Jacob, their father, and to him, Joseph, his son.

And all of the brothers wept torrents of tears
    They regained one another but had lost too many years.
How greed and envy corrodes the soul
    And breaks into pieces a soul that was whole.

JACOB'S LAST WILL AND TESTAMENT

Jacob called his sons to him and said, "Gather about me so that I may tell you what will happen to you in the future. Reuben, you are my first-born, my might and the first fruits of my strength, the excellence of grace, and the superbness of my power. Because you went to your father's bed and made it impure by lying with my wife you lost your rights as first-born. Gen XLIX, 1–4.

Jacob's beard was ragged; his breakfast stuck to its hairs.
    His voice was thin but resolute as he called together his heirs.
They gathered 'round his bed to hear him speak his last.
    What they feared the very most was he'd review their past.
Don't strain yourself dear father they whispered to silence him
    As they gazed into his eyes already growing dim.
But Jacob trumpeted each word into each anxious ear.
    What he said was loud enough for posterity to hear.
Reuben, my eldest, proud and strong,
    You dishonored my bed and did me wrong!
When I think of what you've done wrath rises within me
    And I will never forgive and never set you free.
You lay with your brothers' mother for gratification's sake,
    Your destiny will be paltry because you played the rake.
I had expected much, much more of my very first;
    Now forever, Reuben, you are damned and you are cursed.
        Reuben received no pardon for his heinous deed,
        Jacob-Israel expected virtue from a son who one day would lead.

Simeon and Levi, you are killers, acting out your rage
    Neither Reason nor Justice would either of you assuage.
You and your descendants will be scattered in a holy land
    Just as summer winds scatter shifting grains of sand.
        The brothers objected to what their father decreed;
        But Jacob-Israel expected virtue from sons who would lead.
Issachar! Jackass, brawny, brainless son
    You'll be a slave to everyone.

Zebulon! You will live by the sea
> Commerce will be your destiny.
>> To their fates these brothers without question did accede;
>> Jacob-Israel expected virtue from sons who one day would lead.

Dan! You are cunning, fit to rule
> Be fair and just, act not a fool.

Gad! You're a magnet to those who waylay.
> You will pursue robbers and drive them away.
>> Although no mantle, a fitting fate they agreed;
>> Jacob-Israel expected virtue from sons who one day would lead.

 Asher! Your land will grow the food for the table of a king
> And a bountiful harvest each year to priests you are expected to bring.

Naphtali! You are handsome and fleet as a deer
> And will sire children of deep beauty not just veneer.
>> Happiness and beauty will mark their breed;
>> Jacob-Israel expected virtue from sons who one day would lead.

Joseph ! God will bless you with all His Mighty Powers
> And will give you water, cattle, children, grains and flowers.

Benjamin ! You are like a vicious wolf, wily and strong of will.
> Morning and evening you'll hunt, then devour the kill.
>> Jacob-Israel had no worries that these brothers would others feed;
>> Jacob-Israel expected virtue from sons who one day would lead.

Judah! Judah! Clever as a fox; strong as a lion,
> Your name will be praised forever in Zion.
>> Jacob-Israel had named the son whose virtue did exceed
>> His very own and would the patriarch succeed.

"Children of Israel, forever," sighed Jacob with his last gasp of breath
> But before his thought had ended, he was embraced by Death.

To wrestle with God was to be Israel's bequeathed estate
> And wrestling with God has ever since been his children's fate.

ISRAEL'S PLIGHT IN EGYPT

And there arose a new king of Egypt who did not know of Joseph. And he said to his people the People of Israel are too numerous and powerful. Let us deal with them smartly. Exod I, 8–10.

Joseph ben Jacob was soon forgotten
    And the gains of his kin, though fairly gotten,
Were despised by Egypt's newest ruler
    Whose reign was even crueler
Than marauding jungle cats
    Ripping prey in their habitats.

As the world around contentedly slept
    Israel's Children lamented and copious tears wept.
Egyptian whips delivered their thwacks
    One after another upon their backs.
The lashes making bloody prints
    Caused God on High to Cringe and Wince.

How Israel moaned; how Israel groaned.
    "Abandon us not in this hour of our needing,"
        Israel prayed as their wounds were bleeding.
            Then into history, a moment dark and grave,
                Arose a Moses his people would save.

MOSES IN THE ARK OF BULRUSHES

And when (Moses' sister) could no longer hide the infant she took him from an ark of bulrushes and glazed it with slime and pitch and put the child in it and placed it at the river's edge. She watched from afar to know what would happen to him. Then the daughter of the Pharaoh came down to bathe in the river and sent her handmaidens to fetch the ark. Exod II, 3–5

The Hebrews sojourned in Egypt for many years.
    Food was abundant; water was clean.
Life was good; neighbors were friendly.
    Few were their cares; few were their fears.

Then a Pharaoh arose, a man of bitter bile,
    Who knew nothing of Joseph or of his kin.
Seeing the Hebrews prosper, he proclaimed,
    "Drown all Hebrew boys in The Nile."

There was a couple to whom was born
    A beautiful boy with complexion swarthy.
Perplexed were they as to how to save their child
    And from their bosoms to have him torn.

Yocheved, the mother, built a bulrush ark
    And covering it with pitch so it would not sink.
With tears scalding her worried face she set down the babe
    And watched the ark float into the dark.

A wind came up and the trees swayed;
    The river rippled and the ark bobbed.
The infant cried himself to sleep
    As the ark slowed and strayed.

From shore to shore the ark did drift
    It was stopped by Pharaoh's daughter
Who studied the sobbing child
    And from the ark did she him lift.

Now Miriam, the boy's sister, was waiting nearby.
    "Your majesty," she asked,
Will you breast-feed this Hebrew child?
    The princess answered, "Not I. Not I."

"I will find a wet nurse, if you agree."
    The princess said yes and Miriam rushed
To her mother and said, "Our Moses can be saved,"
    If you the wet nurse will be."

So it was. And Moses learned ways of royalty,
    And became an Egyptian prince.
But to the nation of his birth mother,
    He never forgot his loyalty.

HISTORY OF THE EXODUS FROM EGYPT

And God said to Moses, "Pharaoh is willful; he refuses to let My people go."
Exod VII, 14.

In the Holy Scrolls there is engraved
    The story of a people once enslaved
By an Egyptian Pharaoh who without remorse
    Inflicted pain with a brutish force
On the innocent Children of Israel
    Who cried in misery but to no avail.
He ordered their healthy as well as their lame
    To build red fires of the hottest flame
And to bake him sturdy bricks
    From a clay and crushed straw mix.
This ruthless Pharaoh then decreed
    To shape the bricks with greater speed.
And those who worked no faster
    Were whipped on the back by a cruel task master.
How they did lament and wail
    When Pharaoh commanded each Hebrew first born male
To be found and killed
    And the blood of the babes to be spilled.
Decrees like these wore away their pride
    And a furious rage arose inside.
They prayed, pleaded, and humbly appealed
    But Pharaoh's law was not repealed.
What Pharaoh's men did instead
    Was to beat the Hebrews until they bled.
He also multiplied the brick making quota,
    Their tormenting pain mattered not one iota.

Anguished cries rose throughout the nation.
    Pharaoh called it "insubordination"
And provided even less food to eat.
    "I am a god," he said with great conceit,

"Whatever I do is right and just
    And The Children of Israel must in me show trust."
He was uncaring of their lack of food
    And turned his back in a vengeful mood.
As Pharaoh continued to shout and curse,
    Living conditions grew even worse.

There had been born under Egyptian noses
    A Hebrew son called "Moses."
Drawn from the river by Pharaoh's daughter
    He was taken from his ark floating in the water.
She had him schooled in a princely way:
    He studied law and how to pray.
He felt the pain of each brick cutter
    But bit his tongue so's not to stutter.
In his heart, though, he truly knew
    There was something that he must do.
"Save us God!" he would pray,
    Not just once but three times each day.
As Moses' prayers reached God's Ears,
    The Almighty's Eyes Stung with Tears.

MOSES AT THE BURNING BUSH

And the Messenger of God appeared to Moses in a flame of fire in the midst of a bush and when Moses looked he saw the bush had not burned. And Moses said, I will turn aside to view this spectacle. He understood not why the bush was not scorched. And God Called to Moses who said, "here I am." Exod III, 2-4.

While walking one day Moses had seen
    A Bush Aflame but Yet Stayed Green.
He stopped and stared.
    Then became quite scared

When a Voice Austere
    Breathed, "Draw near. Draw near.
I have a Plan Our People to Save;
    No people should suffer the fate of a slave.

You will know this very well,
    And Israel will for generations retell
That from this land you will them lead."
    This is what God, The Merciful and Just, Had Decreed.

But then Moses, a person humble,
    Said, "O God, I'm afraid my tongue will stumble."
Then God Replied, "I'll Help you carry
    This heavy burden. So no longer tarry!"

LET MY PEOPLE GO

And Moses and Aaron went to Pharaoh and announced, "the God of Israel Said, release My people so that they may go into the desert and prepare a feast in My Honor." Exod V, 1.

Without pretense Moses appealed to Pharaoh
    "Let my people go. Let my people go!"
At first the Pharaoh did agree and even gave his guarantee.

PHARAOH CHANGES HIS MIND

Pharaoh ordered his overseers to demand the slaves gather their own straw to make bricks. Exod V, 7.

On a whim Pharaoh changed his mind
    And increased the work he had assigned.
So Moses went to The Pharaoh, and spoke in a voice quite polite,
    O Mighty father, Benevolent Pharaoh! Let my people go. Relieve their plight.
Pharaoh said looking him eye to eye, "Moses, My princely son, I'm in a fix.
    I ask you who will the mortar mix?
I have this dream to populate Pithon and Ramses,
    Two cities to scintillate with solar rays.
Moses interpreted Pharaoh's dream,
    And said "Father forget your scheme.
My people came here briefly to sojourn
    Now it is time for their return
To their God-Promised land.
    You must understand.

PHARAOH DID NOT LIKE MOSES' REPLY

God said to Moses" I will stiffen Pharaoh's heart because he refuses to let My people go and I will send scourges upon his house. Exod VII, 3

Such words Pharaoh could not bare, his heart grew hard as a granite rock,
    And plagues came from everywhere before Moses led out his
        flock.

SO PLAGUES VISITED EGYPT

Behold, God Said My rod will smite the water and the river will become blood. Exod VII, 17

The plagues befell the Egyptians of old
    And punished them a thousand fold.
There were locusts, rains, and rivers of mud
    And water that tasted of human blood.
They suffered from boils and then from lice;
    Vermin devoured all of their rice.
Millions of frogs upon them preyed
    And daily darkness despaired and dismayed.
Flies swarmed around their beaded brows
    And murrain spread to their dairy cows.
One plague all of their crops did destroy
    And the last plague slew each first born boy.
Slaying Egypt's first-born sons ended its tyranny
    And Moses exclaimed "At last we are free. We are free."
That night in the midst of a clamor,
    "We leave," he said without a stammer.

THE EXODUS: ONE REPORT

Moses stretched out his hand over the sea and God Caused the sea to go back and made the sea dry land. And Moses raised his hand again and the waters rolled back over the pursuing Egyptians, their chariots, and their horsemen. Exod XIV 21–27.

While the Egyptians slept the Israelites crept from their abodes along bramble roads,
    The eye of the night, their only light.
        Thousands of feet in rhythmic beat
Paced in harmony, rustling like leaves of a swaying tree.
    The young, the brave set the pace; the elderly, the infirm felt out of place
But hobbled on, eyes filled with tears from their pain and from their fears.
    Thus Moses led his people out of Egypt land and led them across the desert sand.
Each day was hotter than the next; tempers flared, all were vexed.
    Daggers of heat their bodies stabbed; fits of thirst their bodies jabbed.
Lice crawled about the hair; eyes ached from the sun's fiery glare.
    Sand fleas gathered under their chins and then would sting their sunburned skins.
Feet swelled and refused to walk; mouths were dry and could not talk.
    Veils of sand hid the skies; sudden sand storms blinded their eyes.
In makeshift graves were buried the dead, never to know woe or dread.
    Weaned babies wailed from clawing thirst;
        the genteel felt shame as their bladders burst.
Desert misery was all around; no relief was to be found.
    Moses felt the barbs of those who railed as well as the pain of those who ailed.
Still he knew he must proceed if his mission was to succeed.
    With deep conviction he said, "Have hope; our future lies ahead."
There were people who wanted very much to believe. But there were others who asked to leave

And return to Egypt where a bed would be a treat and there'd be meat for them to eat.
No matter how hard they might yearn for Egypt, it was too late to return Moses insisted. And the Israelites persisted.
To realize their dream one day to be free they had to spread esprit
Which in their souls they would sow and there would give it time to grow.
So they struggled and they coped and they prayed and they hoped
That soon they would enter the land that Moses' scouts had scanned.
It happened one day under a shining sun that a vision occurred to everyone.
Lightning flashed round a nearby mount.
There were thunderclaps too many to count.
How could this mystery be explained? Is this what God had Ordained?
They thought it must be the Lord God's Wrath but walking down the mountain path
Was Moses aglow with Rays from Above carrying with him God's Rules of love
Carved in slabs of cold, gray stone. Hundreds of rams horns then were blown
To announce the gift Moses was bearing.
The gift which he with the world was sharing.
In a subdued voice that trembled Moses proclaimed to all assembled:
Man, wife, and child of every station in every place and every generation.
"These laws I today unveil will forever prevail
To guide humanity in its passage through life in seeking joy and in avoiding strife.
Every soul was electrified and awed by this bequest from their loving God.
Israel accepted what God had Gifted, their sagging spirits becoming uplifted.
But what they discovered on that very day is that freedom comes to those who stay
The course. In each loving heart beats a promised land
Whether one climbs a mountain rock or treks on desert sand.

Life is a journey beyond the lowly to discover within us what is holy.
We are pious pilgrims all ready to answer God's Silent Call.

THE EXODUS: ANOTHER REPORT

Through marshy highways Moses raced
    According to the Plan that was Traced
By God on high who Was his Guide
    And never for a moment Left his side.

Pharaoh's soldiers were in hot pursuit
    And followed each step of the Mosaic route.
They met where waters were gently flowing
    And rows of reeds in mud were growing.

Lightning branches filled the air
    And thunder resounded everywhere.
The Sea of Reeds then Was Parted
    And the Children of Israel to dry land darted.

And as they reached the drying ground,
    The pursuing soldiers then were drowned.
In the desert Moses' kin felt free
    Just as they dreamed was their right to be.

FOOD FOR THE TRIP

Seven days shall you eat unleavened bread in remembrance of the days when I God rescued you from Egypt. Exod XII, 14. And the people took their dough before it was leavened. Exod XII, 27.

With matzah only, the unleavened bread,
    the Children of Israel from Egypt fled.
Ten drops of wine we toss and spray
    To remember Pharaoh's judgment day
For making Israel lowly slaves
    Then beating them with prickly staves.
The sharp sting of their whips
    Lives in history on our finger tips.

SONG OF MOSES

Moses sang to God, The Highly Exulted. The horse and its rider You Threw into the sea. You Are my strength, my song, and my salvation. I glorify and exalt You. Exod XV, 1–3.

How Mighty is God. Who is mightier?
    How Glorious is God. Who is more glorious?
Who is more Wondrous than God? No one.
    God Guides and Forgives the willful,
Liberates the distressed and Watches Over the oppressed, the hungry,
    the homeless.
    Awesome is God. Magnificent and Majestic is God.

MIRIAM'S DANCE

And Miriam, the prophetess, with timbrel in hand. danced with all the dancing women with their timbrels. Then Miriam sang a song to God, The Mighty and Exalted. Horse and rider were today thrown into the sea. Exod XV, 20–21.

The curtain of heaven wrapped 'round the sun in a golden mystery.
    Another day had run its course and drifted into history.
Lying in a watery grave was Egyptian warrior with horse
    Sentenced there by Almighty God with Sadness and Remorse.

Miriam watched the rolling seas, the moon beamed upon her face.
    With outstretched arms she beckoned to the Light of Heaven's Grace.
Her soul gleamed with the Flame of God, a flute-like voice left her lips
    Giving thanks for victory and for breaking Egyptian whips.

Her voice was reaching distant stars when night breezes gave its call,
    Head held high she stepped in dance, her shadow growing tall.
Then out of every tent there danced maidens on to the sand
    To join Miriam 'neath the moon in a song sublime and grand.

They spread their arms towards heaven as Miriam before had done
    Then circled the mystic prophet and sang together as one,
"Thank You O Mighty and Merciful God, Who our enemy Did Defeat."
    And silhouetted against the moonlit sky they moved to a timbrel beat.

IN THE WILDERNESS

And God Spoke to Moses, thus, I have Heard the murmuring of the Children of Israel. Tell them that at dusk they will eat meat and in the morning, bread. Exod XVI, 11-12.

By day they sweltered in the desert sun; by night they shivered in the chill desert air.
    The relentless winds parched their throats; swarms of gnats matted their hair.
Their starving young stifled their cries; the stoic elderly succumbed to the ordeal.
    The refugees from Egypt wandered into the plague of THE WILDERNESS.

Having punished the Egyptians, God was Careening the Israelites to their doom.
    Moses, Moses the nomads complained our garments are tattered!
Our dreams are shattered.
    Our stomachs have cramps; our kidneys ache.

Did we need to roam this desert to die?
    Weren't there enough graves in Egypt?
    Moses checked his anger, he held back his rage. The burden of leadership was too heavy.
He was caught between a Struggling God and a hurting people.
    God, he humbly whispered, these are hard times.
        There's no food or water.

The Children of Israel, Your people, judge me incompetent.
    O God what can I do?
    They complain and fret. Yet aren't their grievances justified?
If the people You Chose accepted Your covenant,
    why do they now suffer so?
        Do you want them to know that wandering and suffering is to be their eternal destiny?

Zebulon fights with Judah and the families of Judah quarrel amongst themselves.
    Husbands strike their wives; mothers spank their children; and children hit each other.
They are disappointed, distraught, and hot.
    God Replied, I, too, Hear their murmuring.
        Who can foresee every difficulty?

Life is suffering. They suffer and so Do I.
    But there are always solutions, Moses. Tap that rock. Gently! Gently!
Moses whacked it with a great fury. Cool, sweet waters gushed out.
    The Children of Israel slaked their thirst and watered their cattle.

Then a bevy of quail appeared on the desert floor.
    The Children of Israel saw the ruffled breasted birds.
Then the quail whistled, inviting the complaining band to make a feast.
    Are we in the midst of a delusion or is it a miracle?

Two birds ambled toward Moses.
    They did not protest when Moses raised them high and said, Praise be to God.
A desperate mother grabbed the birds and stuck her face into their soft feathers.
    Praise be to God, she cried.
        The wanderers rushed the willing birds.

Grabbing them they sang "Praise be to God."
    They cooked the birds and ate heartily.
    After which Moses led his flock in a prayer of thanksgiving.
When they finished eating some said the birds were there by a happenstance.
    What will we eat tomorrow? and the next day? and the days after that one?
        Moses watched the sun set in a blaze of color and knew God's Power.
            The Children of Israel saw the Glory of God in the rainbow cloud.

MOSES GIVES ASSURANCE

And the Children of Israel murmured against Moses. Oh that we had died in Egypt when we had bread to eat. Then God Said I Will Cause food to come down from heaven and the people shall go out each day and gather a day's portion. Exod XVI, 3-4.

"God will Provide.
    God never Leaves our side.
Moses knelt down in the heat of the day.
    All of Israel heard him pray.
"O Merciful God!" I humbly entreat,
    Our people are hungry. What will they eat?"
He pleaded Do not Abandon us. Watch over us and Grant us sustenance.
    The next morning the fading fog revealed a scalelike matter on the ground.

Manna? What is this? The fascinated but frightened people asked.
    Is it poison? Is this how our "beloved" leader wants to kill us?
    Again they complained.
Is this one of his magic tricks or is it a mirage brought on by our fever?
    A curious child scooped it up and licked it.

His parents, worrying that they their child would die, ululated in grief.
    Scooping another batch the child beckoned to his parents to join him.
"It's like honey," he sang. The onlookers ate and called it a miracle.
    The wanderers, knowing what they had lacked, treasured what they now had.

Then they understood God and smiled but God Understood Israel and Wept.
    But soon they complained to him who led,
        "Tell us how we'll tomorrow be fed."

GOD'S COMMANDS

I am the Lord your God who Brought you out of Egypt, out of the land where you were slaves. I Command that you worship no other gods, honor your parents, Observe the Sabbath, Covet not your neighbor's house. Exod XX, 2–14

But there were more complaints that made Moses despair.
    And he was also aware
That the people he'd led had become unruly.
    And one another were treating cruelly.
So God Taught Moses The Holy Laws
    To stem the growth of human flaws.
These did Moses to the entire people release
    To bring them hope as well as peace.
A Moses descended the majestic mount
    He announced to his people account
Of what God Taught
    Rules to live by what they aught and what they aught not
The animals were silent so were the birds
    As the Israelites gathered to hear God's Holy Words

"I am the Lord Thy God Who led you out of Egypt land.
    Worship not an idol fraud. That is My command!
Never profane My Sacred Name, carry It always in your breast;
    Six days each week are for work but the seventh day is for rest.
Children, honor your parents no matter their age.
    Never do another slay. Always curb your rage!
Do not steal. Do not envy what your neighbors own
    Perform good deeds with modesty; for wayward ways atone!
Husbands and wives adore each other; love your children, too.
    Pass these rules etched in our lore to each generation anew!"

Not a sound was made, the air was still
    As Israel accepted the Lord God's Will.

The earth quaked and the mountain spun
    And Israel proclaimed The Merciful is One.
The laws which You Gave to us today
    We accept and we will obey.

It was then they understood Creation;
    It was then they became to God a nation,
Transformed from a people without an aim
    To one guided by The Eternal Flame.
Each babe from every tribe and every race
    Is born with the Light of Heaven's Grace.
And every person with flagrant flaws
    Becomes pure by heeding God's Holy Laws.

ASCENDING AND DESCENDING MT. SINAI: ANOTHER REPORT

The morning fog rings the mount
    A misty curtain drapes the peak.
So many secrets lie within:
    Enigmas, too many to count.

Each day I see Moses climbing high
    Where The Divine Presence ever shines.
And mysteries lift like the fog
    When he looks into God's Cosmic Eye.

He savors the milk of Torah,
    He tastes its sweet fruit galore,
Then pledges to be God's servant
    Who'd clarify every nebula.

The sun in all its brilliance
    Makes the veil of fog disappear
And glowing with Divine Beauty
    He clutches God's words in a trance.

Like you, I am there at Sinai
    Like you, I am there when Moses descends.
We listen to his messages
    That all peoples dignify.

"Hear! Oh Israel God is One!
    Do you accept God's Law?" He asks.
We kiss the fringes of his shawl
    And take up God's Work undone.

"Teach God's Words to those yet to come
    To generations yet to be.
Teach them with love and diligence
    And God's prophets they'll become.

GOD'S WORDS ENTERED MOSES' EARS

1. Worship only Adonai Who freed you from slavery
    2. Neither fashion an idol nor false gods deify.
3. God's Name is blessed. Abuse it not.
    4. Observe the Holy Sabbath as a day of rest.
5. Honor parents throughout the day and give them your respect .
    6. Cherish all manner of life; never another slay.
7. To your loved ones faithful be.
    8. Never steal.
9. Never accuse another falsely
    10. Never succumb to your passion

Then the Great Teacher's words dissolve
    But their meanings are etched in our souls
And will beat in our children hearts ever more
    With love, with justice, and with resolve.

THE COMPACT WITH GOD

Moses gathered about him tribal elders, commoners, man, woman and child, strangers who joined the camp, wood cutters, water carriers, those present and those yet to come and enjoined them to enter into a covenant to accept God as theirs and to obey the commandments given to Moses at Sinai. Deut, XXVIX, 9 ff.

Moses had awaken as the cock had crowed
    To behold Angels Arriving from their Heavenly Abode
Aglow with a Message for him to air
    And to all God's Peoples for them to share.

He blew the ram's horn with wind from his throat,
    It resonated its melody note after note.
His flock was summoned from here and from there
    To hear God's Words for them to bear.

The people gathered all around
    To hear Those Words gently Resound
To every land and to every race
      To every time and to every place
        To the rich princes and to the abject poor
          To the new born babe and to the mature,
            To sisters and brothers; fathers and mothers,
          To slave and to free, to those present and to those
    yet to be.

    No one on top and no one, below;
      God's Words to all Did Echo
    Because all are the same in God's Sacred Sight
      Whether Priest, Commoner, or the Levite.

Moses said, "Let's all pledge to be Children of God."
    Hearts beat loudly; souls were awed.
"Let's all laud God be we of Abraham by birth or child of Israel by
    choice."

And they sang out in one voice,
> "O wise and merciful God! You Will Be ours
> > And we will be yours.

THE AMALEKITES

And Moses said to Joshua "Select men and do battle with Amalek. And when Moses held up his arms, Israel triumphed; when he dropped them Amalek dominated. And Aaron and Hur held up his hands and Israel prevailed. Exod XVII, 8–16

The midnight watchman fell asleep and did not hear the Amalekites creep
    Along the desert floor to gather where the quail stopped days before.
They came by the tens; they came by the hundreds, hiding beneath their kaffiyad heads
    Which blended in with the wavy dunes. By dawn there were abundant platoons.
The leader whistled; the soldiers ululated and rushed the Hebrew tents unabated.
    At the dawn's morning light, they slashed and burned everything in sight.

The stench of burning flesh filled the air HELP US, HELP US was heard in prayer.
    In minutes infants, mothers, and aged were dead as Hebrew soldiers to war had sped.
Swords clashed, rocks were thrown and Israel's losses had already grown.
    Raise my arms bid Moses, Israel's fate was upon his shoulders.

Why do You God Test us so? Angrily Moses demanded to know.
    Whenever his faith was flagging, Israel's fortunes were also sagging.
But when he realized that men not God wage war his faith in God began to soar.
    Then in a frenzy Israel defeated their foe and buried them in row after row.
The souls of Amalek, though, did not die, but thrive and still brutify
    Israel in the dead of night, ever killing innocents with great delight.

NOT A CURSE BUT A BLESSING

Come curse Jacob, said Balak to Balaam who says instead How goodly are your tents O Jacob; your dwellings O Israel. Num XXIII 7—XXIV 5

Into Balak's heart hot desert winds seared fear
    That the emigres from Egypt, an enchanted people,
Would spread plagues of blood, boils, frogs, and darkness-
    Not to mention the killing of first born sons-
And would overtake his kingdom, destroying his gods,
    Those exquisite creatures devoutly formed of clay
That brought fertility to his people and abundance to his land,
    And victories to his army grand.

Fear spindled into anger and rasps of rage
    As when the heavens exploded with booming thunder.
A call went forth to Balaam, a prophet, an enchanter,
    A holy man who through his curse
Would cast a spell on the people of Israel
    Whose fringéd shawls danced in the breezes.

Fresh from a rebuke from his jackass whom he abused
    And from the True God whom he revered,
Balaam, handsomely paid for his efforts,
    Opened his mouth and clutched his cloak.

Balak waited anxiously to hear Balaam's prophesy.
    The voice was the voice of Balaam, filled with rapture,
But the Words came from the True God.
    The winds carried the prophesy to the four corners of the world.

"How goodly are your tents, you issue of Jacob;
    How magnificent are God's temples.
You will be blessed with fertile valleys,
    You will be exalted among the nations.

> Those who bless you will themselves be blessed;
>> Those who curse you will themselves be cursed."
> Upon hearing these words Balak was mortified
>> And prostrated himself and died .

NOT AS GRASSHOPPERS BUT AS HEROES

And we spies Moses sent to scout out the land of Canaan saw giants and we were in our own sight as grasshoppers. Num XIII, 33.

Twelve scouts had gone to Canaan, one from every tribe had Moses sent,
    And returned months later, reporting how their time was spent.
Caleb said the land that God had Promised to our ancestors one and all
    Was filled with milk and honey and with nuts and fruits that enthrall.
Joshua agreed with Caleb, his words tingled in the air:
    The land had riches many for each of our tribes to share.
Not so, scowled the others. There was nothing inviting about the land
    Because it was a place where giants slept on rocks and washed in sand.
What we saw would terrify those in whom fear dwells not at all.
    To them, and us, we were like grasshoppers whom the giants tried to maul.
But we managed to fly away, we barely got back unhurt,
    Go not to Canaan and harm you will avert.

The Children of Israel trembled; they cursed Moses in their rage.
    Did you lead us out of Egypt giants in war to engage?
Then a Voice came from the winds It Spoke with Words quite clear
    If you think of yourself as grasshoppers your name you will smear.
You Children of Israel put aside your worries and fears
    Your offspring will enter Canaan amidst trumpet calls and cheers.
And so it came to pass the desert children the Canaanite foe had felled
    And entered into the Holy Land.
Among all of the prophets none was more renowned
    Than Moses who by God Had Been Crowned.
His life was closing and no one was more deserving of reward and glory.
    Then God Beckoned to him to appoint Joshua to preserve the story
Of The Holy Writ and to pass it
    To generations to come for them to transmit.

JOSHUA

Joshua was filled with intelligence and Moses named him his successor. The Children of Israel obeyed Joshua and kept the commandments that God Gave to Moses. Deut XXXIV, 9.

"Who me?" Joshua asked, his face beet red.
    "You want to give me the job to lead the children of that unruly mob
Who sinned at the sight of the molten calf. And you want me to lead them on God's Behalf?
    For me that's no task; from me it's too much to ask. "
"Joshua, Joshua, patient and wise, you can the motley tribes civilize.
    Be their leader; God is your Guide. God Will ever Be by your side.
You are Called upon to lead the people to the Holy Land
    And God's Mercy and Justice to teach and expand."
Reluctantly, Joshua agreed.
    When God Calls you to lead, you must accede!
    Together they studied The Sacred Law esteeming each other with profound awe.
God Learned that the One Who Is Sage must learn to Control outbursts of rage.
    What Joshua learned that God's Law transcribed must in every heart become inscribed.
This he taught to his nation for them to teach to each new generation:
    From false gods their errant ways sever and spread God's Sacred Laws forever and ever.

2 The Prophets

The Old Testament is divided into three sections. The first is the Pentateuch, The Five Books of Moses. The second section is The Prophets. It deals with the conquest of Canaan, the establishment of the monarchy and its history, and the oracles of preachers Called by God in each generation to reaffirm and strengthen the ethical teachings of their Mosaic heritage. The prophet bears the burdens of rebuking his people and warning them of impending doom unless they change their ways. At times those messages resulted in physical harm to their bearers. Many a prophet also undertook to comfort his listeners in their woes and to teach and guide them in the path of the higher morality of God's Teachings. The books of the Prophets present a motley array of themes in the Mosaic Kaleidoscope.

THE RED CORD

Then Joshua dispatched two spies with orders to secretly explore the Land of Canaan, especially the city of Jericho. When they came to the city they spent the night at the dwelling of the prostitute Rahab. Josh II, 1. This is what you must do to be saved said the spies hang this red cord from the window, the very one from which you let us down. Josh II, 18.

> Joshua sent two scouts to spy out the land and report to him what they saw firsthand.
>> Into the city of Jericho they furtively crept as the unsuspecting citizens languidly slept.
> But they had not gone unseen crawling about in a rugged ravine.
>> Soldiers chased them in quick pursuit. But the scouts, chosen because they were astute,
> Escaped into the house of Rahab, an Ishtar whore, who hid them in flax stalks on the attic floor.

Soldiers came to Rahab's door shouting, "Surrender the strangers, sodden whore."

She said she knew nothing of spies; she only knew games where she was the prize.

The soldiers snickered and heartily laughed, Rahab was known well for her exotic craft.

She told the soldiers to check her grain sacks and the attic floor where she stacked sprouts of flax.

Would spies be hiding there? The soldiers doubted and were caught in her snare.

The soldiers departed, chagrin in their eyes, and sang," she plays games where she is the prize."

Rahab hid the spies for three whole days; she knew many soldiers and their crafty ways:

They'd give up the search in a day or two and would change direction and scout anew.

Rahab asked the spies to spare her kin an ill fate when Joshua's army razed Jericho's gate.

On the window of your house hang a cord of red, the spies told Rahab as they fled.

The spies were saved thanks to Rahab's advice and told Joshua their findings precise.

Joshua prepared his band to leave, Jericho was the goal they were to achieve.

Priests dipped their toes into the Jordan River; the waters stopped, not even a quiver.

Then they their rams horns mightily blew and crossed the dry river bed with much ado.

For seven days they marched around until the walls of Jericho fell right to the ground.

Jericho surrendered to the soldiers of the Lord and Joshua stretched out his shining sword.

This land we bless in God's Holy Name; this Land of Canaan in God's Name claim.

Joshua's men saw a cord of red and spared Rahab and kin who gave the the spies bed and bread.

In Israel she lives to this very day as a spirit of virtue who had once been a stray.

SISERA AND YA-EL

Sisera ran from Barak to Jael's tent. He pleaded give me something to drink. As Sisera slept, Jael took a hammer and a tent peg and drove it through his head into the ground. Judg IV, 14–21.

Sisera of Canaan addressed all his men: Israel had abandoned their God again.
   Now is the time to strike at its heart- they swagger about thinking no one's as smart.
The captain heard cheers rise from every side, thousands men stood there bloated with pride.
   Nine hundred chariots were ready to fight and utterly destroy every Israelite.
When we win, and what I say is true, an Israelite damsel for you each, maybe even two,
   That's how the booty will be divided- in Sisera's mind the war was already decided.
The men ululated as they rode, thoughts of deeds heinous overflowed.
   But God's Heart with Hot Rage was Filled that Israel by Canaan would surely be killed.
Now was the time for Israel to unite; Now was the time tribes to join the fight.
   But Reuben tended its sheep; Dan sailed the ocean deep.
Asher stayed by the coast; Gad was in business deeply engrossed.
   Deborah, a judge of uncommon courage, of wisdom of remarkable mintage,
Found Zebulon and Naphtali unafraid to die, fearless to look any foe in the eye.
   Barak was called upon to lead the corps; he was uncanny in the way to wage a war.
Barak with three hundred men fleet as does defeated thousands of the marauding foes.
   Sisera escaped and bolted into a tent begged Ya-el for water, his energy spent.
She fed him milk and curds of cheese, a sign of friendship which set him at ease.

Then as he lay asleep in his bed Ya-el pounded a peg into his head.

His death was instant, there was not even a sigh, the way every brave soldier hopes to die.

His form had been perfect a moment before; now it was lifeless, just debris of war.

What wisdom he learned drawing his last breath is how fragile is life and how final is death.

Now in the hereafter where soldiers tread Sisera staggers with a peg in his head.

"Ya-el killed me," he moans in disbelief, But Ya-el answers not, bathed in grief.

And his mother awaits him, late to return, and vexes that ill tidings is what she will learn.

Her maids gathered 'round her to say Sisera's dead, lying in state with a peg in his head.

She rent her robe and loudly keened, my son is no more, his mem'ry's demeaned.

What good is a son not living but dead and six feet of earth over him spread?

Deborah and Barak their victory granted, a requiem to all fallen then sadly chanted.

YOUR GOD IS MY GOD

An inscription found at Ugarit states that we, the Children of Israel, say to you, Children of Canaan, that your god, the age´d sovereign of the pantheon, El: Merciful, Benevolent, Creator, Kadosh, the holy one, is our God.

GIDEON, THE DELIVERER

And God Commanded Gideon, "Go with all of your expertise and deliver Israel from the Midianites, settlers in Canaan. I Am Sending you." Judg VI, 14 Then Gideon testing God again said, "Don't be Angry with me; let me speak just once more. Please let me make one more test with the wool. This time let the wool on the threshing floor, be dry, and the ground be wet." That night God Did that very thing. In the morning the wool was dry, but the ground was wet with dew. Judg VI, 39–40.

   Israel whored after alien gods once more and a Fiery Wrath from The Eternal did Pour:
      How can I Wipe away the sinful stains of those whose ancestors I Freed from chains?
   To stop the spread of moral blights, God Delivered them to the Amalekites,
      A marauding tribe who inflamed their lives and sliced off their heads with hunting knives.
   As if the cruelty of Amalek had not been enough God Offered them to Midian, a tribe as rough.
      Year after year the formidable foe was wrecking the crops Israelites would grow.
   People starved and babies died; and the Merciful God and the Angels Sighed.
      "Hear, O Israel," God Summoned them all. But no one answered God's Sacred Call.
   Yet God Heard their moans wherever they slept; and Angels watched over as God Had Wept.
      On bended knee they pleaded to God upon Whose Laws they had trod,
   "O Merciful God Save the innocent; Wait not for parents to come and repent."
      God Considered their request. "Find Me a man of virtue!"
   Then began a Quest.
      Angels Searching throughout the land Found a humble man, one who could take command.
   Gideon! Gideon! He is the man to lead Israel's people and enact God's Plan.

Angels Looked into Gideon's face and he saw in them God's
  Holy Grace.
"Gideon! Adonai is with thee, You have been chosen to set Israel
  free."
  Hearing God's Name, his heart fluttered "B-Blessed is His Holy
    N-Name!" his lips stuttered.
Gideon was neither a coward nor a knave, an errand from God
  required someone brave.
  Arguing with the Angels, he asked, "Tell me why we are suffer-
    ing so under God's Watchful Eye.

Did not You God Almighty set Is-ra-el free
  From Egypt's cruel hand and made a covenant to give us this
    land?"
God Answered not his question but Said "There is nothing to fear;
  there is nothing to dread.
  By your side I'll Be and victory is yours and you'll put an end to
    murderous wars.
Gideon, unconvinced, tried out this test, he placed fleece on the
  ground that God had Blessed.
  In the morning on that very spot the fleece was wet but the
    ground was not.
Dare Gideon fated to lead Israel's men test the Lord once again?
  He petitioned God to reverse what He had done and in the
    morning when rose a fiery sun
Shining through a rich azure sky the ground was wet but the fleece
  was dry.
  Gideon declared, "You are God, The True." but he needed brave
    men the foe to subdue.
Ten thousand volunteered to drive out the foe, a force of that size
  could deliver much woe
  But could also suffer many losses. His strategy called for a clever
    process:
One with an element of great surprise to be done by a force of a
  smaller size.
  At the river's edge he ordered his men to drink water like dogs,
    though, did not think

What was the purpose of this test and noisily drank thinking this was a jest.
  Those who quietly like a dog had lapped were the ones who Gideon tapped.
Three hundred lappers formed companies three. Upon Gideon's signal they went on a spree.
  Each man broke a pitcher and sent up a flare and blew rams' horns with a cracking blare.
Down the mountain at night they sped and startled the enemy asleep in bed.
  Chaos broke out. The foe ran east and west, many in circles, alarmed and distressed.
Wherever they ran Israel's men pursued slaying thousands until Midian was subdued.
  But the tribe of Ephraim chastised Gideon, the hero, who had just vanquished Midian.

"Cousin, we were there to help. Why not ask?
    What's the matter, weren't we up to the task?"
  Gideon replied it was God's Proposition to Send them on a more important mission:
Midian's kings to capture and behead; Ephraim's face was saved; its anger had fled.
  Gideon asked how can *my* grapes compare with Ephraim's vineyards, rarest of rare?
Their pride swelled; their fury quelled.
  The triumphant Gideon returned to his vines and devoted to God a thanksgiving shrine.
Then the people sought a man who could lead, a man of great character, of exceptional breed.
  Gideon was offered a regent's ring but refusing he said only God Could Be king.
Grudges grew in jealous minds and flour of hate its grain mill grinds.
  Among Israel there was growing unrest; among the very people whom God had Blessed.
Gideon, now aged, no longer quelled a moody spirit which in Israel dwelled.

>Despaired and defeated Gideon then died.
>>What he united had become untied.
>In time, Israel's ways again became flawed; forgotten again were Moses, Gideon and God.
>>Perplexed Angels Wept in grief as They Watched war rob lives like a gluttonous thief.
>Vexed Became the Heart of the Lord; upon seeing Israel worship the edge of the sword.

JEPHTHA, THE DELIVERER

Jephthah, a skilled warrior, was born to his father's amour. His brothers said he would have no share in their deceased father's bequest. He fled . When there was trouble in the land, the leaders of Gilead sought him out and said "be our leader to fight the Ammonites." He said you forced me from my father's house but if you take me back God will Give us victory. Judg XI, 1–11

   Son of a whore, son of a whore, leave this house forevermore!
   So spoke to him Jephthah's brothers, offspring of different mothers.
      Through forest and field Jephthah roamed to build for himself a hearth and a home
      Relentless had been their searing refrain splattering agony throughout his brain.
   Son of a whore, son of a whore, leave this house forevermore!
   His mirror showed him to be a miserable clod. Then he turned for help to God.
      Within him rose a valor supreme that restored and rebuilt his self esteem.
      Each day he worked his grove and vine and offered thanks to God Divine.
   In time he wed and a daughter was born whom with fatherly love he did adorn.
   Again the soldiers of Ammon attacked and Israel's defense again was cracked.
      Desperately, the Elders of Gilead sought Jephthah out. In their minds they had no doubt
   He could his soldiers lead and in battle would clearly succeed.
   "Didn't you call me son of a whore and did you not my spirit gore?
   "Forgive our cupidity," they replied." "It was stupidity. Have mercy! Our children have died.
      "Lead us and Ammon's ruthless bands will be mush in your expert hands."
      Saddened by the fate of his kin Jephthah took command determined to win.
   First he tried to negotiate with Ammon's king, a peaceful settlement for all to bring.

But the king refused to agree and Jephthah and his men went on a spree
    And soundly defeated Ammon, the foe.
        But Jephthah felt an offering to God did owe.
    "The first creature to come out my door, I will offer to God," he swore.
Who should it be but his own little girl, who greeted her father with a swirl and a twirl.
"O father dear." she sang growing near. "You've safely returned," and gave a loud cheer.
    Isaiah why weren't you born centuries before to make a change in Israel's lore?
    Burning flesh is not how we thank God nor do we give thanks by brandishing a sword.
A pure heart doing good is how God is praised.
However, Jephthah knew this not and sacrificed his belove´d daughter he had raised.

    As they had done to Gideon before the men of Ephraim, like lions let out a roar,
    Why weren't *we* asked to join the fight, do you think that we are afflicted by fright?
But Jephthah *had* asked for their aid. "Not e'en when in your grave you're laid,"
Had been their surly reply as they spat in Jephthah's pleading eye.
    He reminded them what they had said and in revenge struck them dead,
    Leaving trails of blood on Israel's past, not for the first time nor for the last.

SAMSON, THE DELIVERER

The wife spoke to her husband saying "A Messenger of God, awe inspiring, came and said to me that I am to conceive and bear a son. Have no alcoholic drinks and eat no impure foods for the boy will be a Nazirite to God from womb to death. " Judg XIII 6,7.

Sadness fell like icy winter rain upon the house where joy was slain
> By a silent killer who nightly crept into the bed where Manoah slept

With his wife of many years, who among Danite women had no peers
> In piety or in devotion to God. Yet she felt it very odd,

And could not be reconciled, though beseeching God, she had no child.
> The silent killer lurking in the night, with its craving for smiting gametes at their site,

Had not quenched the fire of passion's flame, although that had been his deliberate aim.
> The childless couple were inspired to learn what it was that God required

For sperm and ovum to meet by chance and within the Danite's gates to do their dance.
> Lost in reverie on one Sabbath day, as she 'neath a fig tree sat to pray,

A Stranger Approached as in a dream Whose Face was Radiant and all Abeam
> With a Divine glow. A mother you will be within a year. Wait and see.

Eat pure food only and drink no wine your child will be consecrated to God Divine.
> But you must take special care never to cut his golden hair.

He will be steadfast as the sun that shines and he will vanquish the Philistines.
> The neighboring Philistines were a mighty foe, schooled in war they inflicted much woe

Upon the men and women of Israel and in many a battle did prevail.

The woman did as the Stranger Said and made a child with the man she wed.

The child was fleet and canny and strong but decided for himself what was right and wrong.

He was stiff-necked with a willful streak whom women for pleasure was wont to seek.

The women he sought were not of his kind but enchanting Philistines with spells that bind.

To Manoah, his father he spoke man to man and laid before him his marriage plan:

I have found a woman of comely hue, her smile beckons and she is soft as a ewe,

Her hair is curly like ocean swells, and about her neck are perfumed smells.

Her body is lithe like a swan in flight and her eyes my heart with yearning ignite.

When I gaze upon her flawless face, my knees buckle and my heart would race.

Samson felt faint from professing his love, the woman he cherished: his darling, his dove.

Father! Go to her father to ask for her hand! But Manoah refused Samson's demand.

He said, find a wife from your own kin! In rage Samson smashed jugs that perfect had been.

He returned to Philistia to marry his love but a turn of fate gave him a shove.

The father of his bride to be had given her to another secretly.

Samson trusted this man who blinked a smile behind it was hidden his wile and his guile.

Samson's temper flared and he killed the men he saw, yielding to passion, his villainous flaw.

Filling the field was corpse after corpse; flooding his heart were pangs of remorse.

O God why must we our neighbors kill? O God why must they our blood spill?

If the game of life is "we must kill first" then civilization will be doubly cursed.

Samson was brooding for many a day; then Delilah winked at him as she passed his way.
    Once again his heart was racing and he longed for the woman that he was facing.
She kindled the flame that fled from his heart; she excelled in love's secrets and practiced its art.
    Samson was amazed at the heights he rose to and thought he found love, honest and true.
But as she her fantasies did intricately weave she devised a plan Samson to deceive.
    Tell me Samson, she whispered in his ear; tell me Samson, tell me my dear,
What makes you so strong?
    My hair must not be cut; it must grow long.
That's what makes me the very best. With arrogance he confessed.
He disclosed his secret at a moment weak- as she kissed his lips and caressed his cheek.
    She cut his curls one night as he slept; then Philistine warriors about him swept.
With a hot poker they burned out his eyes. Black to him became the blue of the skies.
    To celebrate, a banquet was made in Dagon's Temple where they built a stockade
And to its pillars Samson's hands were bound tight; no one saved him from his abasing plight.
    With ebbing strength he drove the pillars away and the Temple of Dagon began to sway.
Ceiling and walls came down with a crash. There was a fire; left only was ash.
    The dying Samson spoke directly to God, why did You Choose me, a bungling clod
Afflicted with strength, lust, and rage, to end my days like a blind bird in a cage?
    Witless I stumbled into Cupid's lair where my soul was shredded and now is threadbare.
God Examined the temple that had been laid waste where evil men perished as well as the chaste.
    "This was not the way for you to die; yet great heroes act bravely and never ask why."

WHAT'S HER NAME, THE LEVITE'S CONCUBINE

A Levite dwelling in the other end of the hill country of Ephraim acquired a concubine from Bethlehem. One day she left him to go to her father's house. Her husband went to get her back. After finding her, the man set out to return to his home. The two stopped at a house overnight, some men pounded on the door and said send out the man so that we may have our way with him. Instead the Levite threw out his wife. They raped her repeatedly. Toward morning she returned and knocked on the door. She was lying at the entrance with her hands on the threshold. "Rise," he demanded. She did not reply. He placed her on his donkey and when he arrived home he cut the concubine in twelve parts and sent them to each tribe in Israel. Judg XIX, 1–30.

What's-Her-Name, the Levite's concubine, ran away to her father's house in Bethlehem
    Where she wandered in craggy hills among the bleating sheep
In utter empathy with them: face to face, breasts to breasts, womb to womb.
    Blithely bounding before the sacrifice, how little they knew the fate awaiting them.
She lifted a skipping lambkin, and cradled it in her arms, gently caressing its oily coat
    Beneath the azure skies, as she was once loved and caressed,
When What's-His-Name, the Levite from Ephraim,
    Who had pursued her and wooed her, now subdued her.
What's-His-Name, her man, was bringing his skipping ewe back home
    And she held the lambkin in her arms as a mother does her belove´d child.
Together they hiked the sun baked trails to the land of Ephraim,
    A smile shone on What's-His-Name lips
And leaden resignation lay in What's-Her-Name's heart
    And contentment filled the lambkin.
Travel weary, they knocked at the door of an old man
    At Gibeah in the land of Benjamin, hoping for kindness.
The old man invited them in. As hospitality to strangers required,

He gave them food and drink, washed their feet, and fed their
  donkeys.
Then there came a banging on the door. The town flotsam shouted,
  "Send out the man, the Levite, so that we may empty our passion inside of him."
Incensed, the old man refused.
  Ye men of broken commandments, he bellowed,
    This is no way to treat a son of Israel, a guest, a direct descendant of Moses himself.
The base scoundrels, heady with desire
  And energized by the shouting of their increasing numbers to do treachery,
Demanded the Levite for their pleasure.
  The frightened husband flung What's-Her-Name to the cowing crowd.
She felt their claws ripping her robe and their paws tearing her thighs.
  One after another they defiled her; one after another they tortured her;
One after another they spat and cursed her.
  What's-Her-Name did not plead for mercy but begged for Death.
Anger, compassion, fear, impotence collided like stormed-filled clouds,
  Lightning scudded through the labyrinth of the Levite's mind.
"O God! Stop these roguish Benjaminite whoresons!
  And I will offer What's-Her-Name's beloved lambkin as a sacrifice to You."
With each thud, each scream, each sob rising from What's-Her-Name's body,
  What's-His-Name, the Levite, thumped his chest in rhythm with his pulsing heart.
He, too, screamed and sobbed. He, too, felt pain. But how could he know *her* pain?
  What's-Her-Name, the Levite's concubine, shivered until dawn.
Then Death wrapped Itself around her like a warm, safe blanket.
  Gleaning the last wisps of life scattered about her body,

She crept toward the door and weakly knocked on it. When the door opened, she bleated, "baa!"
    And fell into the loving arms of Cherubs who Winged their way to an endless forever.

The distraught Levite held her body, sliced it into twelve parts, one for each tribal elder.
    To assuage his guilt, he sacrificed What's-Her-Name's lambkin to God.

An estuary of history flows with blood that reddens the shores of innocence to this day.
    And from the far reaches of Eternity can be heard the sweet bleating duet, "Baa!"

ELI'S CONFESSION

Hannah was deeply distressed, crying bitter tears, sitting by the door of Eli, the priest, she made a promise to God. If I give birth to a son I vow that I will dedicate him to You. I Sam I, 9–11;

Moving her lips she was praying silently and with devotion. Eli thought she was drunk and said stop making a drunken spectacle of yourself. I Sam I, 13, 14.

>Eli's voice, gnarled with age, twisted his name from his lethargic tongue,
>>"Sa-mu-el! Sa-mu-el!" and Samuel came following the voice twisting and tumbling
>
>Against the concrete walls in the silent night desperately trying to stay aloft.
>>The lone lamp coaxed shadows of Eli's disfigured body onto the ceiling.
>
>A whirl of moths hoarded the meager light. Samuel softly spoke to the silhouette
>>Rather than look at Death Whose stench was spiraling in his nostrils.
>
>"Grasp my fingers," the ancient croaked.
>>"When I am gathered to our fathers
>>
>>Make a sin offering for me: a bullock without blemish
>
>Because I had not been without blemish."
>>Samuel writhed in his chair.
>>
>>Who was he a mere acolyte to minister to the master?
>
>Eli's tears were staining Samuel's fringéd shawl.
>>"I lived my life off the sins of others, like a leech.
>>
>>I wanted so to be holy but the smoke of the olive oil in that lamp is more pure.
>
>I hid my sins from everyone but from God. Before you were born
>>I accused your mother of being a drunkard.
>>>Not just accused her but chastised her
>
>With all of the anger my heart could pour out.
>>Would I have been as severe to a man?

But she *looked* like a drunken woman. A cataract of rage rushed
    from my lips.
But I had misjudged her. Little did I know that Penina, your father's
    other wife, badgered her,
    Taunted her. She called her names: cow, pig, slop.
Your dear pious mother, Israel's Hanna,
    Rocked, muttered, and fought the pain of the snake sucking the
        marrow of her soul
And injecting it with disdain. I judged her on what seemed to be
    Rather than what truly was.
        And this coward whose gaze you now avert
Did not admit his error, too filled was he with false priestly pride.
    Our people expected me to be without blemish. Still The
        Almighty Rewards the virtuous
And unlocked your mother's womb. Upon your birth, as pledged,
    she consigned you to God.
    You, Samuel, paradigm of righteousness, carry God's Name.
Never did you perform service for personal gain.
    Never did you oppress the destitute.
        Never did you set before God's holy altar
A swirling, drunken prostitute. But my sons did.
    Coward that I am, I did not repudiate them.
Against my wishes they carried the holy ark into battle
    And I did not stop them. The Philistines slew them
Then scattered their blood on the ark.
    My own sons set a bad example for Israel; priests should be held
        to a higher standard.
You, Samuel, are what is best of the tribe of Aaron.
    Now I have confessed all;
        May God Grant me amnesty. Eli's body twitched convulsively
As the Celestial Messenger clasped Eli's knobby fingers.
    His time had come.
        The dimming vision in his eyes surrendered, the sagging sounds
            swimming in his ears
Were released to roam at random, the wobbly words languishing
    on his tongue were muted.
    Hand in hand they strolled toward eternity.
        Samuel prepared the sin offering.

> A flame consumed the unblemished bullock then curled back
>> toward heaven
>> Following the path Eli trod to meet the waiting God.
> Answering to the higher law of decency
>> Samuel cleaned the detritus of life expelled by Eli's dying
>> stomach,
> Washed the corpse, dressed him in a shroud, and then buried him.
>> Praising the Name of God, Samuel bathed and purified himself
> And was holy in the sight of God and Israel.
>> And Eli was gathered unto his people in peace.

THE PHILISTINE'S PANIC

Samuel told the people of Israel to return to the One True God, "get rid of all alien gods." "Pray for us Samuel," the people replied, we have sinned. Samuel sacrificed to God a young lamb and burned it. The Philistines charged but were foiled and ran in panic. I Sam VII, 5- 10.

Again, the people of Israel were enticed by false gods.
    Samuel called them together and said,"Cleanse your souls.
Worship sincerely the One True God, Creator of the universe."
    Humbly apologizing to God, they consecrated themselves to the One True God
With all their hearts, with all their souls, and with all their minds.
    But at that sacred moment Philistine kings mounted an attack upon them.
"Samuel, Samuel," they pleaded. "Pray for us or the seed of Israel will wither."
    As they fasted to cleanse their hearts of their sins
The heavens shook with crashing blasts of thunder.
    Mountains rocked; waters rose; the skies became black as pitch.
Panic broke out in the Philistine camp. Soldiers ran away,
    Others, awed by the God of Israel, prostrated themselves before Samuel, the High Priest,
And dedicated themselves to serve the One True God.
    And there was a time of peace between Israel and its neighbors.

SAUL BECOMES KING

And Samuel said to the people, "Here is the man that God Has Chosen. There is no one to compare to him." I Sam X, 24

    Samuel wandered from village to village bringing with him the word of God.
        Towns once prosperous had been pillaged by the marauding Philistines.
    Many sheep and milch cows were slaughtered for sport.
        Fields of grain had been torched for amusement.
    Too often did a family mourn an innocent child hunted and slain like game.
        Butchery was rampant throughout the land. Corpses and carcasses covered the landscape;
    The stench of refuse and decay filled the air. Samuel's mission was to offer comfort
        To the bereaved and mercy to anguished souls and to make Thanksgiving offerings.
    But what was there to be thankful for? Grain had been burned; cattle lay dead;
        Houses keened in mourning. Where Was God?

    The Children of Israel were unsettled. From Dan in the north to Beersheba in the south
        They struggled with one another: Ephraim wanted to tyrannize Judah;
    Joseph's tribes bickered with Simeon; and Ruben taunted Gad.
        The Philistines, Amalekites, and Canaanites were strong.
    The children of Israel were weak, scuffling with one another:
        Stealing one another's women, plundering their lands, besmirching their souls
    And all in the Name of God. Samuel silently prayed with a purpose
        Echoing in the caves of his heart, undistracted by the raucous chatter of the birds,
    Or the crackling leaves; noticing neither the blue of the skies nor the fluttering gilded butterflies.

> He closed the gates of memory and hid its ghosts and scintilla in the dark mazes of mind.
>
> Invisible to himself Samuel prayed that the dying soul of Israel be reborn,
>
> That he could learn wisdom to comfort the forlorn,
>
> And that he build a nation that will serve God's Holy Mission.
>
> Then God's Thoughts Grew in every part of his body
>
> And he saw the numerous cell shapes and locations
>
> Become one body crowned by God's Holy Law.
>
> Samuel awoke transformed.
>
> Tears streamed helplessly from his cheeks.
>
> For had he not spoken to God and had not God Answered?

The children of Philistia, suckled on hate at their mothers teats,
> Were again ready to do battle with their immortal foe. Samuel called the elders of Israel

And told them of his vision. Israel would become one nation,
> Great, admired, holy, and united under God's Glorious Crown.

Saul of Benjamin, the least of the tribes, would be loaned by God wear the crown.
> A tumult followed. The tribe of Benjamin exulted; the elders of the other tribes protested.

Why Benjamin, the most insignificant among Israel?
> Shouts of anger and shouts of joy sparked like clashing swords,

Sending snaking splashes of fire into the dark corridors of history.
> Samuel anointed Saul's head with oil and proclaimed him king in Israel.

Saul rallied his kinsmen's rage and marched into battle against Philistia.
> The Philistines were subdued.

Both friends and foes lauded Saul, King of Israel. But Samuel lauded God, King of The Universe.

DAVID AND GOLIATH

Goliath shouted at the Israelites. You slaves of Saul choose one of your men to fight me. If he kills me my people will be your slaves. Saul and his men were frightened. Jesse said to little David take this food to your brothers. David took his shepherd's hook. picked up several stones and flung them at Goliath. One hit his head and Goliath fell down dead. I Sam XVII, 1–5.

'Twas the middle of a summer's day, the sun above was very hot,
   When Goliath shouted across the field, "Send me the best you got."
The Hebrews were not cowards but Goliath was a giant to be feared,
   So they retreated a bit to strategize when through the brush appeared
David, a shepherd, a teen age lad, very short at that,
   Who knew Goliath was strong though crude from the way he spat.
So when next the giant thundered in words terribly impolite,
   "Come out you scummy cowards!" Little David stepped into sight.
Goliath laughed a giant's laugh, "You gotta be kidding me,
   You sent this little whelp who barely reaches my knee."
Goliath and David were face to face the gigantic and the small
   But David stared into the giant's eye, not afraid at all.
David drew his slingshot and gave a stone a ride,
   Which pierced the head of Goliath who fell down there and died.
Jews are not a warlike group; they study day and night
   But when their lives are threatened they must go out and fight.
And even though they're little, and like David, tend their flocks,
   They always sing their psalms to God but also carry rocks.

DAVID REFLECTS ON HIS GREAT GRANDMOTHER RUTH

Boaz and Ruth married. She gave birth to Obed who married and became the father of Jesse. Jesse became the father of David who later became king of Israel. Ruth, 4, 13–17.

   O Ruth, mother of mercy, you *chose* to renounce Moabite ways
      And the Laws of Moses to accept.
   The holy Sabbath you faithfully kept
      And sweetly sang psalms to God in praise.

A FRIENDSHIP FORGED BY GOD

Jonathan's soul was riveted to that of David. Jonathan loved him as he loved himself. On that day Jonathan an David made a covenant with one another. I Sam XVIII, 1–3.

Jonathan looked inward to his soul
    And found it empty hollow and void.
Tall and handsome the prince knew he was not whole.
    Then he beheld bantam David and was overjoyed.
Crowing mutely, he saw the Golden Sparkling Spirit of God
    Beaming from David Circling his own soul in an orb of love.
It was a stunning moment and the prince was awed
    Because David was a Gift to him from God Above.

Jonathan, placid and strong, was enraptured,
    His heart galloped, his knees grew weak.
The boy from the pasture his every fiber had captured
    Despite his youthful physique.
Psalms to God exuded from David's tongue
    In words of uncommon flavor,
Words that were meant to be sung
    Were spiced with artistic savor.
Jonathan soul flowered with mercy and with grace;
    Ecstatic, he sought to enfold every man
With a warm and heartfelt embrace
    Unknown since the world began.

Each admired the other
    No man was a superior
Each pledged to be a brother,
    No man was an inferior.

Two souls blended into one,
    In a union of trust
Which God Mercifully had Spun
    To last till each would turn to dust.

They made a pact sealed with a kiss
    To look after one another
And they discovered unparalleled bliss
    Knowing for each there was no other.

Then there came one sad, sad day
    When David learned his friend was killed in war.
With eyes misted over David knelt to pray
    For the soul of a comrade he would always adore.

Magnified and Glorified is God's Holy Name!
    You Loaned me a friend for too short a time.
Still Your Infinite Greatness I will ever proclaim
    Your Everlasting Mercy is for all a Perfect Paradigm.

SAUL TRIES TO KILL DAVID

One day an evil spirit seized Saul. He sat in his house spear in hand and David was there playing his lyre. Saul flung his spear at David who sidestepped it. The spear stuck in the wall and David ran away. I Sam XIX, 9–10.

Saul languished in his bed, sure that by dawn he'd be dead.
    His mind sunk into the blackest mood, he refused to eat any kind of food.
He reviled David all through the night; no one understood his dreadful plight.
    Not a wink could he sleep; awake all night he'd weep.

He was moaning; he was groaning.
    He cursed; he burst
With rage, unbecoming his station and age.
    When his servant rushed to his side; "You are dissatisfied.
What troubles your majesty?" Saul replied, "I am in agony.
    My mind is in turmoil; my subjects are not loyal.
I hear them murmur against me; I hear their calumny.
    Saul has killed only a thousand of the foe; but upon ten thousand David inflicted woe.

Thunder vibrates in my mind pell mell; lightning sets a fire in my brain I cannot quell.
    David, David is the cause; he broadcasts all my flaws.
Look a him; he's so small. Why is that maggot beloved by all?
    I once stood very erect; now I am downcast without respect.

Everywhere *his* courage is flaunted and *my* cowardice everywhere is taunted.
    Send the scoundrel to me" he demanded; "bring his lyre" he commanded.
David sang a soothing melody and displayed his poetic artistry.
    "No, no," Saul hammered. "Too, too l-l-loud" he stammered.

David tried a different tune to make Saul swoon.
> Instead an impulse seized Saul's gloomy mind, one that made him morally blind.

He threw his spear at David's head, hoping to fill David with dread.
> But David dodged the speeding lance as he gave Saul a tender glance.

Rather than risk regicide, David ran away to hide.
> Saul sunk deeper into an abyss for he had not killed his nemesis.

SAUL'S DECLINE AND DEATH

At once Saul fell down and lay on the ground, frightened at Samuel's prophesy. He was weak because he had not eaten day or night. I Sam XXVIII, 20-21

    Saul lay in his bed forlorn watching clouds hide his star.
        He tossed and turned 'till early morn when he heard Philistines from afar.
    He had not been victorious for some time. He had suffered many a defeat.
        No longer was he in his prime, his heroism was largely deceit.

    Thoughts like these filled his brain, gloomy was his mood
        Weighed down with Israel's pain, in anguish did he brood:
I never achieved a thing in life as father, soldier, or king.
        I had no love for my wife; I sundered everything.

    He left his bed wet with fright, wildly pacing like a lion
        Who in Israel knew the plight of the king of a divided Zion?
And why was Samuel in such a rage? I don't understand his contempt.
        For *God's* Honor did I the battles wage; no priestly role to preempt.

    And Jonathan and David, friends of the heart, how I loved them both.
        I did not want to tear them apart; they had sworn an oath
To each other of loyalty. But they cheated me and my beloved Jonathan is dead.
        And David, that jackal, is free to rule Israel in my stead.

        God Departed from the king's side and the Philistines defeated the men Saul led.
            On his javelin Saul then died and the Philistines cut off his head.

RIZPAH GUARDS THE DEAD

Saul's concubine Rizpah, spun sackcloth to shelter herself from the hanging corpses of Saul's offspring and she remained there until the harvest began. During the day she chased the birds away and at night she protected the remains from wild animals. II Sam XXI, 10.

    For three years that David reigned there was a famine explained
        Only as that which God Had Willed because of the Gibeonites Saul had killed.
    To appease the families of those who fell, and the root cause of the famine to expel,
        David approached the Gibeon folk and these words to them then spoke,

    "What would soothe your injured pride?" They replied, "avenge the ghosts of those who died."
        David asked,"How shall I proceed? "Give us seven men of King Saul's seed.
    Saul who in a frenzy a javelin had seized and whose dark mood David then had eased
        Now lay dying, his name defamed, groaned as his offspring were profaned.

    For David agreed to the Gibeonite demand to destroy Saul's seven kin like contraband.
        They strung them up in the scorching sun and stabbed their bellies one by one.
    The corpses lay moldering in the cold and heat until Rizpah arrived with sackcloth sheet.
        Weeping she covered the slaughtered ones including the bodies of her very own sons.
    She chased the vultures when the day was bright and chased the beasts who prowled in the night.
        She guarded the corpses, victims of crime. No merciful act is more sublime.

AMNON AND TAMAR

Amnon told his cousin, Jonadab, I'm in love with Tamar, sister to my half brother, Absalom. His cousin said, "Pretend that you are sick and go to bed. When your father visits tell him to send Tamar to take care of you. And David did so and Tamar went to Amnon who insisted that she come into his bed. "Don't force me to do such a shameful thing," she said. But he heeded not her pleadings. After defiling her Amnon was filled with hatred for her.   II Sam XIII, 4- 15.

Ahinoam, the least of David's comely wives, knew that a woman like her survives
- Only by heaping love upon her son, and by forgetting the king who would her shun.

And so Amnon, the son, was indulged every whim, and thought himself born of Cherubim.
- Around the palace he haughtily swaggered and drank all night until he staggered.

Handsome, desirable, a gift to the world. And before every lass was his maleness unfurled.
- There was a lady fair for whom he pined, a virgin who was to the palace confined.

He thought of her as a snobbish prig; and she rated him loathsome, below a pig.
- To David, one day, he cunningly feigned a sickly face, one that was pained.

"Father, dear father! Send me cakes sweet and my sister to wash my feet.
- David ached for his son swooning in ennui; to Amnon's sly plea did his father agree.

David sent Tamar, an innocent flower, whom Amnon then did overpower.
- He grabbed her and wrestled her onto his bed; Tamar was frightened and filled with dread.

There was she taken while screaming "stop!!!" But she could not
>   dislodge him so heavy on top.
>   He yowled and yowled with wanton rapture; again and again he
>   did her recapture.

Pressing and jabbing he drummed at her door and biting her face
>   he called her a whore.
>   She pleaded stop defiling your sister and staining her name
>   And filling our house with disgrace and shame.

Amnon just laughed and chased her away beating her like some
>   dog, some wandering stray.
>   Her innocent body with his venom was filled; her sadness and
>   grief could not be stilled.

In mourning, she rented her dress and ashened her face in deep
>   distress.
>   Dazed and distraught she wandered away, thinking of ways her
>   half brother to slay.

Stunned she meandered here and there, remembering in horror her
>   shock and her scare.
>   She reached the home of Absalom, her brother, they were issue
>   of the very same mother.

Absalom had guessed what had occurred and a surge of rage within
>   him stirred.
>   But to his sister he wanted a comfort to be, a source of love and
>   kindness was he.

"Little sister no wrong have you done, you are purest of women
>   under the sun."
>   He washed her face and combed her hair and they joined their
>   hands to offer a prayer:

Comfort us, O God, amongst Zion's oppressed. Her sad tears dried
>   as she lay at his breast.
>   Many years later while shearing their sheep Absalom killed
>   Amnon in a drunken heap.

ABSALOM'S REVENGE

Absalom insisted to David that Amnon join him in the sheep shearing festival. He then prepared a royal feast and told his servants to notice when Amnon was drunk. They did so and he gave the order to kill Amnon and they complied. II Sam, XIII, 23-29.

When the news of Amnon's death arrived David was distraught
He had already forgiven him for all the shame he had brought.
    Absalom, Absalom, Absalom, my son. How miserable my state had been:
    One son, dead; another, fled and my face is filled with chagrin.
Like a bird of prey you perched at the gates and pounced on any opportunity
To humiliate me, your father, Zion's king, and sow slander and seeds of treachery.
    You were planting rebellion and with malcontents conspired
    Then anointed yourself king in Hebron and were in royal dress attired.
How could the country resist your charms: strong, handsome, and most clever of speech?
But thousands were killed because of you as you my monarchy tried to breach.
    I ran away when your men were approaching and then before all my people's eyes
    One after another you took my concubines and shamed me 'neath the bright blue skies.

The people were saying that Zion was yours.
Upon entering Jerusalem you claimed the king's whores.
    As palm fronds sway in the wind and the moon shines through the night;
    Chariot horses stomp on the dead and the dispersed mob you incite.

    And you, Absalom, too, are among the dead, your cause has sped to oblivion.
    Now for you I sit and grieve. Absalom, Absalom, my beloved son.

Then a plaintive voice rose from the grave "Forgive me, father, against you have I sinned."

And David's eyes welled up with tears then he banished the ghost to the wind.

DAVID'S FINAL MOMENTS

When David was about to die he called Solomon, his son, and gave him his last directions. Be confident and do what God Said to Moses and whatever you do you will succeed. I Kgs II 2- 3.

Gravely David wrapped himself in his shroud, soft and white like a downy cloud.
    He was musing about his final rest, his soul rose high like an ocean crest.
His life had been one long blessing and now his lips were expressing
    Thanks to the God Who Called him to lead and without Whom he would never succeed.
Golden light had been his domain but now and forever darkness will reign.
    As his life was ebbing away at the close of the Sabbath day,
Pictures of the past flashed wildly in his mind: joy and pain together were entwined.
    A raucous laugh rose from his throat, remembering battles where he the foe smote
With a band of untutored men: debtors, runaway husbands, and those with a yen
    For risk. Imitating hyenas they raided desert tribes and doled the booty, wrote his scribes.
Then a picture came that froze him with fear. Saul threw a javelin, narrowly missing his ear.
    Then he asked "was my modesty virtue or guise?" Bungling sword-girding seemed wise.
Of course, he knew how one girds a sword but Saul his betters had always abhorred
    And to be on the good side of his superior would defer to them and act like an inferior.

But that was Saul's failing! Unknowingly he, himself, was derailing
    His kingdom, his reign, and his power were unraveled like a petal plucked flower.

In another flash David was a youth again admired by women and praised by the men.

Handsome he was as he strutted about: an ardent lover though sometimes a lout.

Bath-Sheba! Rare was she. Rising in passion who better could innovate the lovemaking fashion?

Palm trees swayed as their hearts quivered; he stroke her braids and their bodies shivered.

Rapture rose to heights unknown; for one moment with her he'd surrender his throne.

Crowding his mind now were Jerusalem's hills whose mystical beauty gave him the chills.

Cheering voices proclaimed him king and commoner and prince together did sing,

"David, David king of Israel You will live forever. It is you we hail."

Those fervent cheers were ringing in his ears

When a rage surged throughout his brain that howled and stormed like a hurricane.

There were voices, more than a few, saying that he, David, was no authentic Jew.

Ruth, his saintly grandmother, Moabite ancestried, took with gladness the Jewish creed,

Upon her they spewed calumny and blame though her Judaism glowed like The Eternal Flame.

Devout she was and truly pious, more righteous than those bellowing bias.

Must zealots never be satisfied until they have others vilified?

Now unfolding before his eyes was the new map of Israel of magnificent size

It began at the Euphrates and ran to the Nile. His pocke'd face filled up with a smile.

He had done it all through diplomacy and war; now Judah's lion could lunge and roar.

Then came a picture with fading fringes- which his stalwart eyes with tears unhinges.

"O Jonathan, devoted friend, I wish I could have reversed your unlucky end."

Tears rolled down his craggy cheek and words were lacking for him to speak.
Then darker grew the pictures he saw painted with anguish and filled with flaw.
He saw lots of killers and lots of dead; was there another way to write history instead?
"Why must it always be written in blood. Why can't its beauty unfold from a bud?"
Widows, orphans, maimed, and blind the costs of war to humankind.
Is all this heartache and pain for naught, is it all just in vain?
He once put this question to Solomon, his son, the wisest of men, barring none.
This reply before his father he spread: "It's true of the ignorant and of the well bred.
All is vanity. That is no mystery. Nothing's new under the sun is human history.
The meaning of life can be learned from the goat leaping craggy ledges to fill up his throat

And when he reaches the mountain top he retraces his steps searching grasses to crop."
The Angel of Death came to David's bed as David was setting his crown on his head.
The Angel Stopped in Its Tracks, just like any loyal subject reacts.
"Lord," David began, "You Have my shepherd Been, and though I wandered into sin,
You Showed me the righteous path to walk and Are now Bringing me back to rejoin Your flock.
I do not fear what is to come; who is able death's meaning to plumb?
But Your mercy will a comfort be today, tomorrow and for eternity."
Then the Angel Wrapped David's soul in a Shawl and David heeded God's Final Call.

DAVID, DAVID BELOVED KING

David, David beloved king.
    In your memory we daily sing
Your psalms that reach heights sublime
    That is not defined by divisions of time.

Brave you were and comely too.
    With a love of God did you imbue
Our people then and yet to be.
    And today we walk with dignity.

Imperfect you were as we all are
    But also of righteousness were an avatar.
David, David beloved king.
    To your memory we'll ever sing.

SOLOMON, THE WISE

Solomon was anointed king, succeeding his father. In his lifetime he was known as brilliant. He formed alliances with many kings and peace prevailed. This poem illustrates his wisdom.

Solomon prayed to God for good sense
    For his mind to his people to dispense.
When there arose in his kingdom
    A difficult problem to solve his wisdom

Burnished by God's Light that shone
    On him, he became the loadstone
Toward which one with a problem would turn.
    In the darkness of mind was he a lucent lantern.

Two women came to him one day,
    Each claiming to his dismay
And on her honor each had sworn
    To be the true mother of a newly born.

But who was the true mother was Solomon's dilemma.
    He meditated over Moses' Torah
And ordered his staff
    To cut the baby in half.

"No give the child to the other!"
    Urged the true mother.
But Solomon the wise,
    Seeing tears streaming from the woman's eyes,
        Awarded the babe to the mother true.
        And the other woman in shame withdrew.

THE MISSION OF AMOS

Amos, a shepherd from the town of Tekoa, was Called to prophesy two years before the earthquake during the reigns of kings Uzziahu of Judah and Jeroboam of Israel. These spoke these words:
   God Roars from Zion;
      And Screams from Jerusalem;
         And the pastures of shepherds shall waste away;
            And the crest of Carmel shall wilt. Amos I, 1–2.

Amos wandered fields tending his sheep when God's Pained Voice Rose from the deep.
   Lightning sizzled in his sea-green eyes and gilded streaks sped through clear, blue skies.
Then a Voice, Caring, Strange and Remote, nettled Amos's reticent throat
   Where it quivered and vibrated and with every word humanity berated,
"Amos, Amos how Sad Am I that so many brutify
   My Creation and turn it into an aberration.
Instead of showing justice, nations afflict the needy;
   Instead of showing kindness, the rich are greedy.
Amos call them by name! Each of them are in shame!
   Edom, Ammon, Philistia, Moab, Gaza, Tyre, and Syria.
But Israel and Judah, who accepted My Laws, are themselves paragons of flaws.
   How they once made My Heart with joy Leap but now they make My Eyes Weep.
Justice, justice is the duty of every nation. In My Eyes there are no differences of station.
   And, now to My chagrin, destruction awaits every one in sin.
"Oh God, my God" Amos humbly appealed;
   "Say to Israel," The Voice Said, "Because you stole from the poor their bread
And adorned holy alters with ill-gotten gains for sins such as these I'll Withhold Spring rains.
   And the people scoffed, his dire warning to dispel
   And no rain in Israel that year fell.

AMOS SAYS LET JUSTICE REIGN

God Spoke to Amos, Saying, "I Have no use for your religious festivals; I Cannot Abide them! I Will not Accept the animals fattened for offerings. Instead, let justice course like a rivulet and righteousness like a river that never dries up. Amos, V, 21–24.

    Feeding the poor and aiding the weak is the worship sincere that I Seek.
        I speak to you whose ways are flawed; remember Me.
        I am Your God.
    I am the Spark of Mercy in your soul and the Warmth that Flows from burning coal.
        I am the Thrust that moves the wind and the Judge who Sentences those who sinned.

    I am the Lord *all* peoples share; I Listen to every honest prayer.
        But if you My Laws disobey, fire and locusts will be your pay.
    Grain will wither and grapes will dry; mothers will starve and babies will die.
        Foes will conquer and will debase and you'll be exiled to decay in disgrace."
    Silence rippled in Amos deeply vexed, trembling as God's Message he expressed.
        His mouth spoke the Words that he had heard but Israel thought him quite absurd.
    They stoned him and sent him away and into sin they persisted to stray.
        Then the earth shook and mountains quaked; the sun grew hot and the soil was baked .

    Seeds that were planted refused to grow and juice from grapes ebbed its flow.
        Cattle died for want of food and the stench of death did they exude.
    Locusts came and Bethel caught fire and melted in Flames of God's Burning Ire.
        The foe burst through and killed young and old just as God's Words to Amos Foretold .

As Amos the righteous path humbly trod he pleaded and prayed to Almighty God.
    Enough! Enough! Israel has suffered too long. Merciful One Forgive their wrong,
These are Your children, heirs to Your Laws who renounced their sins and righted their flaws.
    Absolve their sins, they do what You Willed; help them Your House with justice to build!

    And God Heard Amos' humble plea and once again Set Israel free.

THE WORDS OF HOSEA

God's Message came to Hosea during the reigns of Kings Uzziah, Jotham, Ahaz and Hezekiah of Judah and of King Jeroboam of Israel. God Said to Hosea marry a whoring woman who will have children of whoredom for the people stray from following God. So he went and married. Hos I, 1-2.

"How can I, God, Cast you off, O Israel; how can I Forsake you. My Love for you is too strong? Hos XI, 8.

> A vision came to Hosea, the Ephraimite seer; a Distant Voice Whispered in his Israelite ear.
>> Hosea! Envoy that God is Succor, Help, and Savior. Speak to Israel about its behavior.
> They have abandoned Me and dishonored My Name;
>> Instead, they the virtues of a sculpted stone gods proclaim.
> Condemn them for their deceit; censure them for their conceit.
>> They swindle; they murder; they drink too much wine;
> Remind them Hosea that I'm the One Who Fattens their kine.
>> They sell their daughters' virtue and they plunder,
> Remind them Hosea that I'm the One to Command the thunder.
>> Ask them who brings the rains that make the grains grow.
> Inquire of them who protects them from woe.
>> Remind them Hosea that I'm the One to Free them from slavery;
> Enlighten them that I'm the One Who Forgives their knavery.
>> Remind them Hosea that I'm the One to Soothe their pain ;
> Enlighten them that I'm the One Who did Creation Ordain.
>> Remind them Hosea that I'm the One Who Created Light;
> Enlighten them that I'm the One to Guide them to do right.
>> Because they dishonored Me, because their priests practiced blasphemy
> Because their judges are unjust, because in Me they showed no trust
>> Their future will be bleak and filled with doom; in strange lands will they dig their tomb.

Hosea listened to God's Angry Spleen vented because Israel made
itself unclean.
> In the hot sun gilding the pillowed hills Hosea spoke words that
> filled him with chills.

Hear my words fellow Israelites!
> Listen to me you who chase delights!
>> In gods of stone and wood have you trusted and after a golden
>> bull have you lusted.

Like me you are wedded to a whore. My wife three children to me
bore.
> Jezreel, my first born, recalls the disgrace of the murders done
> in that place

By Jehu founder of this present dynasty, cursed be its destiny.
> Next, my daughter was called Unloved because the Name of
> God was defamed.

My next child, Not-My-People, a son, Has Been Disowned by The
Holy One.
> Your whore, Baal, leads you astray and from the true God takes
> you away.

Surely it should be clear that Israel was once Held dear
> By God whom you have forsaken. When will you awaken?

Unloved remain not; Not-My-People be not a blot.
> Our God have you profaned; our God have you pained.

Be not like my whoring wife; exemplify fidelity in your life.
> Be loyal to God above, Who Embraces you with Merciful Love.

Must you be stubborn like mules? Must you ignore God's Sacred
Rules?
> God Does not Ask you to slaughter your kine; God Requires
> neither virgin oil nor wine.

God Requires that you by the covenant abide, the code Given
Moses to be your guide.

> At that moment silence reigned Hosea's spirit was completely
> drained.
>> The people of Israel heard Hosea's pleas and immediately fell
>> upon their knees.

They pledged their love for God will be true and false gods they'll no longer pursue.
  The people of Israel sincerely repented and the God of justice then Relented.
God Confessed to Hosea how Angry Was I but how can My beloved Israel I deny?
  With all of their faults they still are Mine; they radiate with light for My sun to shine.
Beloved-By-God be they renamed;
  My-People again be they proclaimed.

THE WORDS OF GOD TO JOEL

These are God's Words to Joel, son of Pethuel. Elders! Pay attention! Dwellers of Judah listen. Has anything like this happened in your time or in the days of your father? Swarms of locusts settled on the crops, what one swarm left the next devoured. Joel I, 2-4.

Hearken to the Words of God Whom your misdeeds Gnawed.
    A Fiery Wrath you accrue; God's Fury is your due.
Yes! You: every man, woman, and child of Judea.
      Seek not a panacea
    For the locust swarms, rolling in like winter storms.
They have your fig trees and vines devoured; they have all new buds deflowered,
    The sheep have no grass for eating and roam about aimlessly bleating.
The animals of the wild wail and cry because the streams they drink from have all gone dry.
    Nation you are filled with woe; loudly, loudly the shofar blow.
As you hear the trumpet blasting, afflict your body with humble fasting.
    Sincerely repent the wayward way; return to God That you betray.
The people prayed with hearts sincere, neither in shallow words nor verbal veneer.
    And God Made the land fertile once more as it had been in days of yore.
Zion again became righteous and chaste and its foes were trapped and laid waste.
    None of the vicious guilty were spared and Zion's soul was again repaired.
To its former glory was Jerusalem returned where The Merciful had once Sojourned.
    And the locusts that our souls had skinned moldered and blew away in the wind.

MESSAGES OF MICAH

God's Words came to Micah who prophesied in the reigns of Kings Jotham, Ahaz of Samaria and Hezekiah of Judah. Listen all you people. God is your Accuser. Mic I, 1,2.

Micah looked about and saw
    Prodigal rich who are mockeries of humanity,
Priests who are parodies of piety,
    And judges who are travesties of justice.
Throbbing at the very heart of the people
    Are self-proclaimed prophets who personify sham ethics
And practice sacred rites for personal gain.
    Enlightened people had slinked into darkness.
Israel and Judah had gone astray;
      their very foundation was in decay.
    Then the Words of God came to Micah.
        How Anguished They Were; how Filled With Hurt.
Judah had abandoned the Divine Concepts; Israel had deserted
    God's Precepts.
    Did they forget Who Freed them from slavery and Who
    Decreed
That their home will be in Zion and Who Gave them the strength
    of the lion?
    The Words of God stirred Micah's soul and from his tongue
    these words did unroll

O ye rich house of Judah! Micah railed. How God Mournfully
    Grieves, Micah flailed.
    You defile the marrow of God's elect.
        From God's Moral Laws do you defect.
    Even the tattered raiment of the poor you crave and their battered bodies you enslave.
        From daily worries they seek release yet you give them no
        moment of peace.
    How haughty are your airs; how self-serving are your prayers.

At the wretched destitute you sneer; thus your punishment will be severe.

You who today are depraved will tomorrow be enslaved.

O ye priests pledged to shun the personal gift do from moral moorings drift.

Instead of disdaining the profane that which is not sacred you ordain.

You who worship greed will find yourself in abject need.

O ye judges who are so easily bribed; the sense of fairness you proscribed.

By the Supreme Judge will you be Tried; the severest decree will be Applied.

O ye false prophets! Micah scolded. You have God's Elect cuckolded.

If they give you no money or food you offer oracles that delude.

You false prophets are a moral blight; your days will soon be as black as night.

And it came to pass that in war Zion was defeated. Then God Saw Zion was mistreated.

And when Zion's sinners repented from severe decrees God Relented.

As God's Anger Abated Zion's foes were frustrated.

Hope replaced despair and sacrifice was replaced, by prayer.

And like Isaiah Micah avowed that with God's Goodness are all endowed.

To all I say let your swords turn into ploughshares and your spears, into pruning hooks.

Let no nation lift up a weapon against another neither against a stranger nor a brother.

Never teach war again. There will soon come a day when

You will sit under your fig tree and you will savor serenity.

A PROPHESY OF ISAIAH

Isaiah was Called in the reigns of Uzziahu, Jotham, Ahaz, and Hezekiah kings of Judah to warn his people of what was in store for them if they did not change their ways. Hear O heavens, listen O earth. God has Spoken. "I reared children and brought them up and they have revolted against Me. O sinful people laden with iniquity you have forsaken God and spurned the Holy One of Israel. Every head is ailing; every heart is sick. Isa I, 1–5

A prophet rose in Zion whose tears filled the Sea of Shame,
    Where he keened "Judah's lion will soon be limping lame."
Isaiah saw storm clouds growing, spreading a fiery rage
    And winds without pity sowing pain without gauge.
There was yet time to alter its selfish, sinful ways.
    But Zion persisted to falter and strayed into exile's blaze.

ISAIAH'S LEGACY

Isaiah's words unfolded in the midst of a frightening dream
    And ghostlike images made him shriek and scream.
He grieved that so many souls were callous;
    He mourned that so many hearts were filled with malice.
Too many were abandoning God's Ways
    And walking around in a self made haze.
His mission was to lead them out of their dark night
    Into the glory of God's Holy Light.
His heartfelt words were of hope and consolation
    His devotion to kindness and mercy, an inspiration.
His warm tears fall upon each aging face
    To purify all with God's Holy Grace.

COMFORT YE MY PEOPLE

God Says, "Comfort ye my people comfort ye. Zion take heart; your guilt is paid off. Isa, XL, 1 ff.

O Children of Zion! How longer, without basis, you suffer.
    How, punished though now free of wrongdoing, you sorrow.
Your foes have swindled you of joy.
    They have defrauded you of happiness.
They dive at you as a lion pounces on prey.
    They suck the marrow of your soul as a louse drains you of your essence.
O My tormented Children turn to Me for solace.
    O Guilt Ridden Children turn to Me for relief.
You have atoned! You are no longer blemished.
    You are no longer tenants of faults, you have been Redeemed.
I am Your Font of Comfort;
    I, God of Mercy, Comfort you My People.

ISAIAH'S VISION

Zion! Your leaders are like those of Sodom! Hearken, instead, to God's Teaching. Denizens of Jerusalem! You are like the scoundrels of Gemorrah! Listen to God's Entreaty. What need Have I of all your sacrifices. I've had enough of burnt offerings of rams, fatlings, and the blood of bulls; And I have no delight in lambs or goats. The scent of incense Disgusts Me. You have perverted New Moon and Sabbath. Both are solemn time. Your hands raised in worship are stained with blood. I do not Abide them. Cease your evil; do good; become just; aid the afflicted; uphold the rights of the orphans, defend the interests of the widow. Isa, I, 10-17.

Isaiah strode up the hill; all was quiet, all was still.
    A crowd gathered in the midday light, under the sun, hot and bright.
God Drew a curtain across the sun, a veil of darkness then was spun.
    Suddenly from the heavens high lightning sticks serrated the sky.
Peels of thunder shook the vale, raining down balls off hail.
    Wrapped in his fringe´d prayer shawl, obedient to God's urgent Call,
Isaiah, trembling, with fear proclaimed God's Message to every ear.
    God Needs no ram to expiate your guilt; God Needs no first fruits on altars you built.
God Needs no offerings of bloodied beasts; God Needs no service of patronizing priests.
    What God's children are Expected to do is to obey Moses' laws anew.
Wash the stain of sin from your hands; take seriously God's Reprimands!
    Worship God with a heart that is pure; maladies of your soul at once cure.
Renounce your evil ways! Denounce the one who slays!
    Steal not from the rich or from the poor! And the ways of false gods at once abjure!
To the widow and orphan be kind and just! To the strangers give your trust!
    Resolutely pursue the righteous path, lest you earn God's Wrath.

Do now what God Commands; to proclaim mercy and justice is what God Demands.
 If you do not this message carry out, if you continue God's words to flout,
Know you that a cruel foe with razor-sharp sword will sweep down on you and you'll be gored.
 The throng shrugged shoulders and walked away; Isaiah left the hilltop in deep dismay.

ISAIAH RELATES A DIFFERENT MESSAGE FROM GOD

Truly, I Comfort you O mortal afraid to die. You have forgotten Your Maker that Stretched out the heavens and Laid the framework of the earth. Isa LI, 12–13.

    God, Distressed, Revealed a Message to Isaiah,
        "Say these words to My people.
    'Zion, Zion. My Dear Land and My Beloved People.
        You strayed and you have paid
    For your errant ways and have become castaways.
        You knew desolation and suffered ruination.
    On every street corner your children lay numb; every kitchen had
        no bread, not even a crumb.'"
        Then Zion repented and God Relented.
    With Tender Consolation God Raised the oppressed from their
        desolation.
        Saying, "I God of all Creation, Author of your nation,
    Wrap you in My Grace; your agony Will I Erase
        Your wounded bodies will I Mend; your afflictions will I End.
    Oo-ree, oo-ree. Awake, awake.
        Hit-o-r'ree, hit-o-r'ree. Rouse yourself.
    Your grief, O Zion, depose; don your festive clothes.
        Look to the rising mountain; observe the shimmering seas
    Raise your voices and sing, 'We find beauty in everything
        You God Created
            Our love for You is unabated.
            We, every prince and every clod, Are Delivered by You
            Almighty God.'"

ISAIAH ENTREATS ZION

O afflicted, tempest-tossed and not comforted. I will set your stones in lovely colors. Your children will be Taught by God and will know peace. Isa LIV, 11-13.

> A tempest rose from Babylon tossing fire balls across the fields,
> > Turning Judea's homes to ashes and melting David's shields.
> Our stomachs ached with hunger; our dreams and hopes were dashed.
> > Our heroes fought with courage; their efforts, though, were smashed.
> Hearken to me Zion, sapphire in God's Sacred Crown,
> > God Returns to Comfort you and you will not walk alone.
> Triumphantly march to Jerusalem! Triumphantly declare God's Name!
> > Triumphantly light Torah's torch and bless Its eternal flame.

THESE WORDS CAME TO ISAIAH

O thou afflicted and uncomforted, tempest tossed. Behold I, God, Will Set your stones in exquisite colors, I Will lay your foundations in sapphires, I Will Make your crowns of rubies, I Will Erect your gates with garnets, and I Will Build all your borders with precious stones. Your children will be Taught by Me. Because Israel is burnished with righteousness. Your covenant with Me was witnessed at Sinai and it will spread My Goodness to every land. And You will glorify My Heavenly Kingdom. Isa LIV, 11 ff

  Although Isaiah was humble and meek; the compassionate God
      Inspired him to speak:
    Oh afflicted, accosted and tempest tossed, without comfort and
      grievously lost.
  Behold I, God of all, Will a "temple" of faith Found in splendid
      colors that will astound
    The eyes from each sparkling gem which nations everywhere
      will admire.
  You, My precious people, dear to Me, have chosen the way of your
      ancestry:
    The Mosaic Laws. It is the path of virtue. Following that path
      you will renew
  My Commandments paramount given to all at Sinai's mount.
    And the love of My Ways will increase and you shall discover
      inner peace
  As will every daughter and every son, blessed by The Holy One.
    Oppression is rampant but never fear;
      the fate of ruin will not be near.
  Foes gathering to do you ill will fail;
      those who assail you will do so to no avail.
    No weapon will triumph no matter how sharply calibrated;
  No name will hurt no matter how hatefully narrated.
    Those were the Words of God:
      Words of Comfort not of the sword.
  Words drawn from Wisdom's Well. Come all.
      Drink and excel in clemency and decency.
  Words for young and for old; Words for meek and for bold;
      Those Words were meant for every man and for every woman.

Those Words were meant for rich and for poor.
> Those are the Words whose merit will ever endure.

Because Torah, Moses' laws, is at the highest level on the moral scale.
> Know this that God has with other nations glorified Israel!

Torah's words are for all peoples in every place and throughout time
> And those who live by them will receive God's Blessings Sublime. AMEN

ZION AWAKE

Awake! Awake! Rise up Jerusalem. You drank the cup of fury from God's Hand and swallowed the liquid that made you reel. Isa LI, 17 ff.

    Zion! Wake yourself, Wake yourself. Jerusalem! Turn your ears to What I Say.
        Listen to the words I Relay.
Too long have you eaten the bread of grief;
    Too long have you been afflicted without relief.
Too long did you the cup of sorrow drain.
    Because you once did transgress, you have known only pain.
Now you are forlorn.
    Now you rend your garments and mourn.
How Can I, Your God, Give you Comfort?
    How can I, Your God, Soothe your hurt?
You, My Heirloom,
    I See your gloom.
You, My treasure,
    Have suffered beyond measure.
Dearest Children, know, too, *My* Agony and Pain;
    Dearest Children, know, too, that from now on I Will Abstain
From Punishing you;
    I Will Cherish you anew.
No longer will you drain the cup of bitterness
    But will drink the cup of My Kindness.
No longer will you eat the fare of affliction
    But will taste of My Redemption.
Cleanse yourself of captivity;
    Cloak yourself in Gentility.
I, The Merciful God, Enfold you Tenderly;
    You, My children, must vow to be true to Me.

TO BE AMONG THE RIGHTEOUS

The Spirit of God is upon me, I am anointed by God to be a courier of joy to the humble, to bind the heartsick, to free the jailed; to declare a year of God's Blessings. Isa LXI, 1-2.

    To make this a better world
        Sing a joyous song to honor the humble;
            Speak words to salve the wounded soul;
                Give food to the hungry;
                      Clothe the unclad;
                            Find dwellings for the homeless;
    Sit by the bedside of the ill;
        Pray for their recovery;
            Be unction to the mourner.
    Celebrate the lives of the deceased, delight in their memories; pass on their legacies;
        Guide the young and edify the old;
            Consider and revise the obsolete;
    Build on the ruins of the past;
        And bear witness to the perfection of this world
            Because our cornucopia is full,
                Our compassion boundless,
                      And devotion to justice eternal.

JEREMIAH'S MISSION

The Word of God came to me. "I Chose you, Jeremiah, before I created you in the womb, I Made you holy before you were born. I Called you to be a prophet to the nations." Then I, Jeremiah, answered. "O God! I don't know how to speak; I am still a callow youth." And God Said, "Do not say 'I am still a boy' But go where I Send you and speak what I Command you. Fear no one for I Am with you to Protect you." Jer I, 4-8.

How can You, Merciful God, Send me on this mission?
    I am terrified of crowds.
  They'll stone me; they'll mock me, they'll sneer,
"Look who God Has Sent to admonish us.
  A child! Someone who cannot wipe his own nose."
Jeremiah! Jeremiah! God Replied, I Chose you when you lay in
    your mother's womb.
  I Sanctified you before you left your mother's nest.
I Guided your growing up.
  I Watched over your entering into manhood.
    You are a holy man, a paragon to all.
You, My prophet, a stalwart sinew, a seer for all nations. I will raise
    your legs to climb high hills.
I Will Open your eyes to witness My Divinity.
  I Will Fill your mouth with My Words
That will echo throughout the generations.
  "Sinners: kings, priests, false prophets, and commoners.
Listen with your hearts to The Almighty, Creator of the Universe,"
  Without faltering Jeremiah continued the Divinely Inspired
    Sermon.
"Remember The Words of God Who Led you out of Egypt, and
    Gave you The Law,
  More wholesome than milk and sweeter than honey,
And Willed this land in which you dwell.
  I speak and the skies tremble with fear; *I* raise my arms and the
    seas swirl with rage.
You, once my faithful bride, are in awe of stone gods carved by man
    and placed 'neath palm trees.
  Know you not that *I* Carved the mountains?

Know you not that *I* Formed the birds that fly and the animals that roam?

In you My people *I* Sowed honesty but reap deception;
In you *I* planted virtue but Harvest corruption;

In you My people *I* Seeded love but Gather vexation.

You have sinned upon the hills; you have sinned by the shores of the seas;

You have sinned in the orchards; you have sinned by the rills.

In sadness I Rent My robe; in mourning *I* Sit Myself low.

Abandon your evil ways; return to the paths of righteousness

And *I* will Grant you My Forgiveness and *I* Will Return My Love to you."

Jeremiah's legs trembled as they stumbled down the mountain.

Before his eyes that moments earlier beheld God, he saw the gathered crowd

With rocks in their hands chanting,"Look who God has Sent to admonish us.

A child! Someone who cannot wipe his own nose."

JEREMIAH REVEALS GOD'S ANGUISH

God Said to me, "Israel will be stripped clean like a vineyard after harvest. Rescue all while there still is time." I replied. "Who listens when I speak? They are a stubborn people. They laugh when You tell me to say that Your Anger against them Burns in me, too." Jer VI, 9-11.

The Hopes of God were betrayed; the Words of God were ignored.
> Zion, an island of mercy surrounded on all sides by God's Wisdom,

Was polluted by the sins of its kings and false priests.
> Girded in sackcloth, God Lamented the demise of The Law of Moses;

Wallowing in ashes, God Mourned Zion's every flaw .
> Again and again God's Words Came to Jeremiah

Whose voice spoke Bitterness and whose message offered Comfort.
> "Show caring for your brother; show kindness to your neighbor. That is My Law.

Do justice unto the stranger; protect the orphan; succor the widow.
> I will Protect you from your foe and I Will Heal your wounds inflicted by your enemy.

Mend your ways and dwell gladly in this sacred land promised to Abraham, Isaac, Jacob, Moses.
> The disease that covers your souls will scab as it heals.
> Sing psalms of praise to God."

The people turned away from his pleas; they scorned God's Greatness with the greatest of ease.
> And their songs perjured God's Glory; and their poems to God were derogatory.

Every brother was a scoundrel; and every neighbor, a slanderer.
> The kings excelled in wickedness; and the priests were unsurpassed in deceit.

Israel was ensnared by its own conceit; Judah was trapped by its own greed.
> Only the poor find comfort in the Ways of God;

Only the persecuted find solace in the paths of peace they had trod.
> And the sun cast no shadows in Jerusalem; and the moon hid its face from Zion.

But the disease covering the souls gushed with pus and did not heal.

No one asked for forgiveness; no one repented; and God, now Silent, was Tormented.

JEREMIAH'S RAPPORT WITH GOD

My sorrow cannot be cured; I am sick at heart. Listen O God! Throughout the land I hear the people complain God no longer Dwells in Zion. The people cry out. The summer is gone and the harvest is over but we have not been saved. My heart is crushed: I am dismayed. Is there no relief to be found in Gilead? Jer VIII, 18..22.

O God! You sent me on an impossible task
    To tell the people to mend their ways
"Jeremiah," they jeer, "your mind is a haze.
    Or maybe, your mouth emptied your wine flask.
"How I wish I had never been born;
    My father I curse.
My mother who gave me to nurse I daily scorn."

Jeremiah's eyes were dark with defeat;
    "All I ever wanted was for Israel to live without blemish."
But his passionate message had not penetrated the ears
    Of his people stone deaf from arrogance.

"O God, my Guardian," he pleaded.
    "If You Do not Intercede on my behalf
Who will? Who cares? Who dares?
    My people call me 'cry baby'."
"How deeply you Suffer for Zion," God Replied.
    "You, Jeremiah, of priestly caste,
Are My prophet and stronghold of the true faith."
Jeremiah could not oust the tears from his eyes.
    God Understood! The people are stubborn.
'Though they were flawed; 'though they flouted The Holy Writ,
    Covenant with Moses, and were unfit
They were to be Forgiven and given a second chance.
    God was the Healer; Gilead was brimming with balm.
And so once more Jeremiah urged the people to change their ways
    And to recite praises to God in a Thanksgiving psalm.

    And God Ministered to the willful
        Through Jeremiah with the Balm of Grace
    Which would their perverse ways erase.
            Once again Israel would the Word of God embrace.

JEREMIAH PLEADS FOR GOD'S MERCY

O God! My Strength, my Stronghold and my Refuge in the day of affliction. All nations will come to You from the ends of the earth and shall say, "our fathers have inherited lies, vanity and things which have no profit." God Chides, "Shall a mortal fashion a god? So I will Cause them to know My hand and My Might; they will know that My Name is God." Jer XVI, 19-21.

    Jeremiah's brain pounded; his heart thumped.
        Dazed, the past swam before him; dizzy, the present staggered
           in his mind.
    His voice cried out in pain and anger to his nation,
        "Oy v'avoy! Woe is me. You lie! Lie! Lie!
    You hand down your lies to every new generation.
        Ignoring the wails of the poor, the hungry, the unclad.
    You scorn the Words of the Holy Text
        Given to our Moses by God."
    Then he sobbed, "O Immortal God, Mighty and True!
        Reveal Your Mercy to this generation anew

    And they will discover the Beauty
        Of Your Glorious Creation
    And find the Strength to build
        A mighty nation

    Based on justice
        Built on compassion
    Fashioned on respect for others.
        Drape them in the mantle of Your Torah."

JEREMIAH ENJOINS THE PEOPLE TO HALLOW THE SABBATH

Thus God Spoke to me saying, "Jeremiah! Go and Stand by the People's Gate through which the kings of Judah enter and by which they leave. Then stand at all of the gates of Jerusalem and announce: Hear God's Words, O ye kings and ye dwellers of Judah . Guard your souls against carrying burdens on the Sabbath day and bringing them through the gates of Jerusalem. Carry no burdens from your houses on the Sabbath Day or do any work. Remember to hallow the Sabbath as I Instructed your ancestors." Jer XVII, 19–22.

>Standing in Jerusalem at each gate
>>Jeremiah entreated passersby, The Sabbath nears!
>>>The Sabbath nears!
>
>Let your work abate.
>>>Shed the millstones that weigh you down
>>>And don, instead, the Sabbath crown.
>
>Be you pauper or prince
>>Merchant or artisan
>>>Priest, Levi, or Israelite
>>Join the upright
>>Who heed the law of Moses,
>
>"Bless the Sabbath and Keep it holy."
>
>Abstain from work and worry; leave your burdens at the portal to the Gates of Sabbath. .
>>Then open your eyes and watch the stars greet the Sabbath;
>>>Then open your ears and hear the spheres sing Sabbath hymns.
>>Then open your souls and let God, The Spirit of the Sabbath,
>
>Wrap you in a mantle of joy, peace, and healing.

THE GRIEVANCES OF HABBAKUK

Adonai! how long must I wail and You will not Hear? We are surrounded by brutality. I cry yet You Do not Spare us? Hab I, 1-2.

O Merciful God!
    Your Ears Are Deaf to our suffering;
    Your Eyes are Blind to our misery.
I weep at our torment;
I wail at our woe.
    We are oppressed
    And we are dispossessed
By the marauding Chaldeans
And by the plundering Babylonians.
    Are their sins less grievous than ours?
    Are their faults less galling than ours?
Humbly do I beg you to Unblock Your Ears and Listen
Meekly do I pray that You Unlock your Eyes and See
    That we despair
    And that we grieve.

O Merciful God! Right these wrongs;
    O Merciful God! Save us.
We embrace You; Embrace us!
    O Merciful God!
I see wicked people prosper;
    I see righteous people suffer.
How can You allow this to happen?
    Where is Your Justice?

O Merciful God!   Will the wicked be punished only in the world to come?
    Will the righteous receive their reward only when they are in Heaven?must we wait so long for Justice?
    Why Not Give the wicked and the righteous their due *now*?

O Merciful God!   We glorify and exalt Your Name;
We rejoice and exult in Your Creation.
For our wrongs we cleanse ourselves in contrition;
Raise us from our oppressed condition!

PSALM OF HABBAKUK

O Merciful God I have heard the news about You and the awesome deeds you have done and I am afraid. Let not Your Wrath Obscure Your compassion. Hab, III, 1–2.

    I know You God! I hear what people say
        That you Abandoned the line of Abraham
    Because of its wicked ways.

    I know You God!
        Even when You Find Fault
    With your Children
        You Forgive them.

    I know You God!
        Even when You are Saddened
    By thoughtless children
        You Show Compassion.

    I know You God!
        What mountains do not quake at Your Presence?
    What seas do not tremble
        At Your Command?

    I know You God!
        You Despise evil doers;
    You Disdain wicked rulers.
        But You Befriend the victim.

    I know You God!
        You Have Been Hiding.
    Come forth and Repair Your Creation;
        Come out and Heal this fragile world.

I know You God!
      Your Kindness is without peer;
Your Mercy is Sincere.
      By Your Strength am I awed.

HAGGAI

When Darius was emperor of Persia, God Gave a message to the prophet Haggai to be delivered to the governor of Israel and the high priest. The people say this is not the right time to rebuild the Temple. Why should you be living in well built houses while My Temple is in ruins? Then God Inspired all the people to work on the Temple. Hag I, 2-14.

"Your homes are luxuriously decorated but My Temple still lies desecrated.
    You have planted much, but your harvest is spare. You have clothing but it is threadbare.
The working man has too little to live on; so many of the strong and the young have gone.
    Now go to the woods and cut down trees and hew stones from the hills, God Decrees,
Get skilled masons and carpenters and My Holy Temple with haste rebuild!"
The people heeded and a splendid shrine from the ashes soared; The Temple was restored.
    No longer was The Temple in desolation, it had been replaced with dedication.
God Blessed the soil with sun and rain and in its season came plentiful grain.
    Once again will Judah be strong; once again will they to Me Belong.

ZECHARIAH HEARS VOICES

When Darius was king God Came to Zechariah and Said, "tell the nation that I Was Angry with their forebears but now I Say Return unto Me." Then Zechariah had a vision in which an Angel Was Riding on a red horse and behind were other horses red, dappled, and white. He asked the Angel what do these horses mean? Zech I, 2-4 and 7-9.

    The voices of Isaiah and Micah murmured in the ears of Zechariah
        And anointed his tongue with the Word of God.
    "Go forth," they spoke, "and say 'Welcome back to Zion
        You who were exiled. Welcome back you who were reviled
    By the Babylonian oppressor. Welcome back victims of the Chaldean aggressor.'
        Tell the children of Israel the Message of God:
    No one is born God's Select; no one is born God's Elect.
        But they who observe the Sabbath, they who worship with sincerity,
    They who walk in the paths of righteousness, be they stranger of this land
        Or an inhabitant of another are My Children.
    Clasp their hands and together ascend the sacred mountain."

VISIONS OF ZECHARIAH

1. Zechariah wandered between the crags, prancing like a goat
    When from his heart a vision sprung that formed words inside his throat.
Horses galloped to and fro as if looking for a home
    And Zechariah asked out loud why do these horses roam?
An Angel riding a steed of red said he had asked God above
    Why Do You still Rage at Judah? Show them, God, Your Love.
And God Replied, their ancestors practiced sinful ways.
    The Angel politely countered but the seed of their seed have not been strays.
The Almighty Relented, seeing the Angel's point
    Told him to rebuild The Temple which the Angels Will anoint.

2. Another vision to Zechariah came in which a man held a measuring stick
    "What do you do? "the prophet asked.
        "Surveying Jerusalem by arithmetic."
Then the Angel Spoke to the prophet to stop the man surveying
    Because God with a wall of fire Will Jerusalem be Arraying.

3. A silent voice called "Zechariah" around the bend comes The Messiah
    To redeem the people of Israel from its torment, from its travail.
Lightning arrows will fly about: black clouds will thunder sprout.
    The mighty king will a donkey ride lowly, meekly, and dignified.
At that time wars will cease and the king will bring about lasting peace
    To nations far and wide over which God alone will Preside.
And every man, woman and child who from their homelands were exiled
    Will wear a crown of gold which will God's Merciful Love Enfold.

THE WORDS OF MALACHI

God Said to the people, "I have always Loved you. But they say ' how have You Shown it?' A child should honor the father and a slave, the master. Now I Am the Father. I Am the Master where is the honor due Me? Remember God is Mighty even outside of Israel." Mal I, 2-6.

> Malachi stood on the top of the hill announcing the words God Had Spoken,
> "I have always Shown My Love for you but you have The Covenant broken.
>> The priests light fires of offering but empty is each word; shallow, each deed
>> I seek prayers that are from the heart not from priestly greed.
> There will come a day when evil will burn like straw
> But the righteous will rise like the golden sun because they obey My Holy Law."

THE VISION OF OBADIAH

Through a messenger God Said to Edom "Because You stole from your cousins and murdered them, you will will be pulled down and your name will be ruined. Obad I, 10.

    A vision came to Obadiah; a prophesy to God's servant.
        O exiles of Israel, remnants of Zion,
    I will gather you from Bavel, and I will assemble you in Sepharad.
        I will reunite you to My people and I will reconnect you to My community.
    Causeless enmity between nations will halt and My children will show charity to one another;
        As it was once was between Esau and Jacob
    As it is between the persecuted and the rescuer.
        Blesse´d are they who reclaim their legacy;
    Happy are they who are restored to their heritage.
        But Edom, offspring of Esau, you have saddened God;
    You have brought sorrow into God's Realm.
        Edom! What kind of cousin were you to jeer
    When your uncle Jacob's children were led off to Babylon?
        Edom! What kind of cousin were you to cheer when Judah's holy city was aflame? Edom! What kind of cousin were you to revel at Judah's misfortune?
        Edom! What kind of cousin were you to murder the remnant and then gloat?
    Edom! What kind of cousin were you to scavenge among the ashes of the holy city?
        You have written your doom in history; you have chartered your future.
    Your punishment is to drink of the bitter cup of misery;
        You are Doomed to vanish from the face of the earth! You will fade like the morning mist.

ZEPHANIA'S VISION

God's Word Came to the prophet Zephania. I will Sweep everything away from the face of the earth away from man and beast, the birds from the sky, and the fish in the sea, I Will Make the wicked stumble and Will Destroy the human race from the face of the earth. There will be no survivors. Zeph I, 1–3

God's Words Roared in Zephania's ears,
    "Judah! I Will Punish your sins and Destroy
  The marrow of your nation: your brave, your valiant, your gallant.
Then Will I Demolish your homes, your orchards, your fields.
  You will lie desolate for years and years; whatever to your eyes appears.
Your dead will be unburied in the streets; maggots will on their remains hungrily feed;
  That is what I, Your God, Decreed.
Wolves shall devour your bleating sheep.
    Thus will be the punishment for your deceit.
  Soldiers will quiver with fear in their armor. Storms of fire will melt your temples;
Darkness and gloom will cover the hills.
    No punishment is more severe."
  The Voice Softened, "I Will Repeal your sentence if you learn modesty from the humble
And you will no longer in rebellious ways stumble.
  Learn virtue from the righteous and My Ears Will Hear your penance.
Once you have your sins confessed cling to the One True God
  Who Shelters the poor and Protects the oppressed."
God's Voice Thundered, "But your foes, wanton weavers of lust,
  Depraved embroiderers of lechery,
    Swiftly and decisively will they be destroyed
      Because God is Mighty and God is Just."
Again the Voice Softened, "A day is coming soon when all nations will worship Me alone

And when Israel, My child, will do no more wrong and no person will another reject.
On that day Judah will instill My heart with song and there will be joyful dancing.
And My children will chant psalms of grace and will My hope for a just world fulfill."

NAHUM'S PROCLAMATION

God is good. The people are Protected in dire times. Nah I, 7.

I will Repay you, Assyria, Declares God. I will Set your chariots on fire. The sword shall crush your enormous beasts And the words of your envoys shall be heard no more. Nah II, 13.

> God of Zion Your people cry in pain;
>> God of Zion hear them complain
>> That You Handed them to the Assyrian foe who threw them in rivers to drown in woe.
> Is this the Mercy of God, The Just, to such villains Zion's souls to Entrust?
>> Life was better in Egypt where we were enslaved. Security, not freedom, had we craved.
> Yes we erred and followed false dreams but a Forgiving God with Kindness Redeems.
>> God Spoke to pious Nahum in a lightning flash, turning Assyrian forests to a pile of ash.
> Zion had made a grave mistake when its God did they forsake.
>> But, God Had Made a mistake as well to thrust Zion's people into Assyrian hell.
> Tears from the heavens were overflowing filling rainbows with glistening and glowing.
>> Nahum, numb from having spoken thus to God, knelt in humility The Just Judge to laud.

THE VISIONS OF EZEKIEL

The visions of Ezekiel may seem strange to us in our day. But mysterious imagery was commonplace in his day. As an exile in Babylonia he must have come in contact with such imagery. Bas reliefs have been found of wild bulls, fanciful animals with serpentine feet, wild birds, winged bearded humans with lion feet, and crosshatched bodies. He may also have had contact with Egyptian deities. For example, Thoth, is represented with a human body and the head of an ibis or a baboon and Anubis, is represented with a human body and the head of a jackal. It is conceivable that Ezekiel abstracted these perceptions and blended them as one does in a dream. What exactly they signify has been interpreted variously by many scholars.

* * * * *

The Word of God Came directly to Ezekiel, the priest, in Chaldea. I looked and saw a stormy wind came out of the north and a great cloud with fire flashing whose brightness like burnished bronze was all around. Out of the midst appeared four figures of the likeness of man (or Adam). Each one had four faces and four wings. The face of a man, a lion, an ox, and an eagle And their feet were straight. Ezek I, 3- 12.

> O God! I, Ezekiel, the priest, had a dream!
>   Not an ordinary dream but a dream agleam
> With Divine Light
>   That almost Blinded my sight.
> It was filled with thunder
>   That almost tears me asunder.
> Blowing from the North was a wind intense
>   Like soldiers marching in cadence.
> But it was a wind
>   Whispering," Israel has sinned."
> Lightning flashed;
>   Thunder crashed.
> In the center of the cloud stood four creatures
>   With the most unusual features.

Four faces had each;
    No face had speech.
Each creature had four wings
    And stood together like siblings.
God Said, "share the news to you I've Passed
    As it does your future forecast."
Ezekiel called out, "Listen!" His people listened.
    As he spoke the images of his dream glistened.

What his mind's eyes saw, Ezekiel beguiled,
    Related his vision to the others exiled
In Babylon from their Jerusalem home.
    Thus began his tome.
"Out of a cloud there appeared
    Four human like creatures. Adhered
To each were four wings.
    So much alike were they like siblings.
Touching one another were their wing points
    Two hands were tucked 'neath wing joints,
Their legs were straight
    They could move but could not gyrate.had the same four faces
        From different mortal races:
One face was of a strong ox, another of a keen-eyed eagle;
    Another was of a mighty lion, and the fourth was of a man quite
        regal.
The creatures appeared in a flaming fire
    Like burning coals acquire.
Amber was their hue;
    Erect they stood like a statue.
Beside each creature was a sparkling wheel
    That gave the vision a quality surreal.
The wheels rose; the wheels slid.
    Whatever the wheels did the figures also did.
The rims were filled with jeweled eyes
    That glittered like fireflies.

Then there rose a Canopy Divine
   Scintillating Radiantly from The Holiest Shrine.
Then The Voice of God I heard
   That Whispered to me the Divine Word:
As You Did in Sinai you said we'll 'obey'.
   Walk in God's Holy Pathway.

Ezekiel spoke his conclusion,
   By false gods rid yourselves of delusion."
And the captives with whom he spoke
   From their doldrums then awoke.
Ezekiel's vision to them was clear
   Lion, eagle, ox, and man God Holds equally dear.
Be they like Angels touching each other
   Or like mortals sister and brother
They radiate God's Presence
   And like the sun Beam God's Brilliance.

I felt God's Presence; God's Spirit Took me to a valley where the ground was covered with dry bones. There I could see many, many bones. God Said, "Mortal one, can these bones come back to life?" I replied, "only You God Can Do that." Ezek XXXVII, 1–3.

In Babylon's hills, Zion's children would fear that their history
      would end and they'd disappear.
   I, Ezekiel, shivered in fright that soon would be quenched
      Israel's glowing light.
Then the Spirit of God Revealing Itself to me, said, child of Adam, I
      Am in great agony.
   Israel has strayed and is not contrite and amongst My peoples is
      spreading a blight.
You, Ezekiel, who from the path of right never strays have always
      abhorred their unclean ways.
   You have been faithful to the Mosaic Law; your God you have
      revered and held in awe.

Therefore, Have I Chosen you to exhort the exiles to abandon the gods that they court.

Then I asked God what words should I say? How can I best Your Mission convey?

Then I looked down from the top of the hill; the sight I saw gave me a chill.

Piles of bones were baked by the sun sentenced by Death to oblivion.

These bones will live the God of Mercy then Said; it is hopeless, said I, they are all quite dead.

But out of a dream filled with mystery skeletons walked into hallowed history.

REVENGE UPON ASSYRIA: AN ACROSTIC POEM

Assyria! Curse´d be your name! Bathed be you in a red, hot flame.
   Carpeted by locusts be all your regions; defeat and death may reward your legions.
Erased from history be your viper face; forgotten in the annals be your every trace.
   Gloom and doom be your fate; hemorrhages will burst from your river gate.
Israel in glory will be homeward returning joyously in song with ardor burning.
   Killers will rampage and will Nineveh loot, liquidating the rich mercantile route;
Mountains will tremble and hills will quake; narrows will crumble and bridges will break.
   Oblivious you've been to the those in need; paradigms you've been of lust and greed.
Quaking hearts their flows will dry, ravaging brains until you die.
   Scarlet bodies will enshroud your wheat and turn the earth to a bloody street.
Unjustly have you nursed your grudges, villainy flowed in the minds of your judges.
   Wanton wrongs went unabated, Xenophobic hate you've consecrated.
Yesterday you basked in power and glory; zoom, now, to a death loathsome and gory.

WHERE HAVE ALL THE PROPHETS GONE?

"Ah" is an ending of many Hebrew names. It means "God." Isaiah means God's savior; Jeremiah, God's loftiness; Zechariah, God's remembering; and Zephania, God's mystery. "El" is also an ending of many Hebrew names. Samuel means God's name; Joel, YHWH is God; Ezekiel, God's strength; and Daniel, God's judgment.

> In their graves the prophets silently lie; in their burial places their remains are mute.
>> For Eternity their words will thunder; beyond Time their voices will sizzle like lightning.
> They are the scruples of morally-starved spirits; they are the decency of ethically-hungry souls.
>> Gathered in their holy places are Isaiah, Jeremiah, Zechariah, and Zephania;
> Assembled in their celestial rewards are Samuel, Joel, Ezekiel, and Daniel.
>> These were among God's Anointed; these were among God's Appointed.
> Simple shepherds and lowly priests; humble craftsmen and modest smiths.
>> One day they were ordinary citizens, no different from others.
> Then a sudden Summons from the Divine Transformed them
>> From reluctant appointees into God's humble Messengers
> And from hesitant speakers into God's eloquent spokesmen.
>> To their eyes was revealed every scintilla of every flicker of every flame,
> Every faint edge of the clouds, every cell of pollen of a flower,
>> Every droplet of sweat between the hairs of a camel's beard.
> In their ears was heard every whisper of the most distant zephyr,
>> Every sigh of the afflicted, every sprouting of every seed, every wave of every heart beat.
> In their hands came balm for healing the destitute, the ill, the shackled;
>> The oppressed, the afflicted, the wronged, and the sinners.
> They were the Reflections Radiating the Mystery of God;

> They Mirrored the Wonder of God and they Reflected the Awe of God.
> They spoke God's Thoughts with pure tongues; they revealed God's Words with chaste souls.
>> Hearken to the Word of God, they'd say; listen to God's Commands, they'd inveigh.
> Do good and not evil; act righteously and not out of malice.
>> God Rewards the virtuous and Punishes the transgressor.
> But they also contended with God to Forgive the wayward
>> And they pleaded with God to Show Compassion to the sinner.
> Their words live in our hearts still; their voices echo in our minds yet.
>> Their authority reprimands our misdeeds but their caring comforts us in our struggles.
> But where are the prophets today?
>> Where are they who fight moral decay?
>> They live within us telling us what is right to do; they lead us in a life that's true.
> Their works are etched in our lore; their words are inscribed in our very core.
>> Their works inspire every generation; their words exalt every nation.
> They are the moral compass whose needle points to God;
>> They paved the path that the righteous of all nations have trod.

3 The Writings

The third section of the Old Testament is known as the Hagiographa or Writings. It is a miscellaneous collection of scrolls read on the three pilgrimage holidays, a fast day, and a day of celebration as well as books dealing with wisdom, liturgy, and history. Two scrolls are scribed to Solomon: The Song of Songs and Ecclesiastes, Kohelet in Hebrew. Ascribed to David is The Book of Psalms. Scholars debate about authorship. What is not debatable is the power of endurance and vitality of the texts. The poems that follow were inspired by these and other sacred texts in the canons of many faiths.

Scrolls on Pilgrimage Holidays

RUTH AND NAOMI

Naomi pleaded with Ruth, "go back home with your sister-in-law." But Ruth answered "Wherever you go, there will I go; wherever you live, there will I live. Your people will be my people. Your God will be my God. They went until they arrived at Bethlehem, The town's people were elated. "Is this really Naomi?" they burst out. "Don't call me Naomi" she replied. "Call me Marah because God Made my life bitter." Ruth I, 13–21.

In her own eyes Naomi was bitter not sweet.
    What travail in her life did she not meet?
   She lived in Moab, strangers to her, where slurs toward her people were often astir.
Her husband was dead; two young sons were dying. In her wrath her wits went flying
   And she disowned God Who had Created a world slipshod.
Thinking these thoughts made her feel shame. Why must God be the One given blame?

Then disease devoured the bodies of her boys like a raging fire flares and then destroys.

Once again was she wed to her pain and a loss of hope inflamed her brain.

A life of loneliness Naomi was to face when Ruth gave her a tender embrace.

"Go home to your own," Naomi insisted. But her daughter-in-law had her entreaty resisted.

"Wherever you go, there shall I follow. Where you nest, there shall I rest.

The God Who is thine, Will also be mine. And where you will die, there, too, will I."

Hand in hand walked the sisters in grief, their love for the other gave each relief.

Arriving in Judea, both women were greeted, warmly welcomed as queens are feted.

This was home their hearts told them so and never again from this land would they go.

Ruth tended to Naomi's every need and looked for work with utmost speed.

In Boaz's field did she barley glean when one day she was by Boaz seen.

His eyes were moist; his heart did melt. Never before had he such passion felt.

Ruth found him kind; someone to admire who rekindled her heart with love's burning fire.

Then one night while the world was asleep Ruth into his tent did quietly creep.

In a moment sweetly sublime into Boaz's bed did the widow Ruth gently climb.

There she lay by his side; her love for him she could not hide.

During the night he awoke to find Ruth, his kin, for whom he had in his heart had pined.

He covered her gently so she'd be warm and quelled the torment which within him did storm.

In the morning when they awoke looking at Boaz, Ruth then spoke, "Take me dear Boaz as your loving bride."

"Forever and ever," Boaz replied.

And he thanked God for The Gift of his wife, she thanked God for renewing her life.

A SONG OF SONGS: THE BRIDE'S BALLAD

Cover my mouth with your kisses. They taste sweeter than wine. Take me to your chamber and there we will delight in love, sweeter than wine. Song I, 1–4.

Blessed art thou O God Who Celebrates life by Bringing joy to man and wife.
Enter my chamber, dear husband, my king! let me hear your sweet voice love songs sing.
    In every corner of my room are lilies-of-the-valley in bloom.
Above my bed Lantana hovers sending sprays of florets ablaze.
    I look into your eyes and see eternity;
        I taste your lips and take in immortality.
Approach me, my dear; my sun, moon, and stars. Draw near.
    How my fingers long to touch your forehead you adoring man to whom I am wed.
I yearn to caress your cheek. I feel my fingers growing weak.
    When you are near I drink at your trough; when you are away your grandeur I quaff.
Gaze upon me with your eyes bluer than the azure-woven skies.
    Look with favor upon my face aglow with the radiance of your grace.
Now my beloved lie by my side let your fingers glide
    About my silver studded pearls bunching my silken-woven curls.
Caress them with your finger tips; nuzzle my neck with your warm, moist lips;
    Kiss my nose, my cheeks, my eyes; kiss my knees, my navel, my thighs.
Unlace my silken gown; be my verb, I am your noun.
    Delight in my femininity; I rejoice in your masculinity.
Lick my lips with your tongue; hearken to my song I've never before sung.
    My heart beats with desire; my breasts are for you to admire.
My nipples are rose buds awaiting your kiss and my soul succumbs to ecstatic bliss.
    Rivulets of rapture from my every crevice flow; in my eyes is a shining glow.

With your fingers nimbly caress my navel gently.
> Let our eager hands meet to trace on my innermost depths words of love so sweet.

Sing to me of bliss; cry out with me in rapture.
> Savor the trembling of my joy so pure.

> The earth is shaking; a volcano is quaking;

Your mystical legacy will I receive as a child together we conceive.
> Such a thrill is known only to man and wife, Blesse´d creators of new life,

In passion we welded; in wedlock we melded.
> Every color of the rainbow is found in couples that sacred marriage has crowned.

A SONG OF SONGS: THE GROOM'S BALLAD

Blessed art Thou O God Who Celebrates life by Bringing joy to man and wife.
Come to me, come to me my love; fly into my arms my queen, my dove.
    The fragrance of frankincense and myrrh fills my chamber with passion de coeur.
How grandly does our love for each other bloom.
    You as my wife; I as your groom.
    Come lie by my side; feel my sinuous muscles my beauteous bride.
Lay your head upon my breast. Listen to the pulsing in my chest.
    My ardor rises with your caresses; my fingers curl your raven tresses,
Spinning pleasures that enthrall upon the border of your shawl
    That you will forever wear covering the silken strands of your hair.
Lets clasp hands upon your chest then twirl circles upon each breast
    Like the orbit of the Earth attending the Sun's daily rebirth.
I bring my sweet lips to yours and my passion soars.
    Then I kiss your hand, the one I caressed and bring it close to my breast.
O love of mine so chaste; I invite your tongue my navel to taste.
    The chamber that has till now been sealed opens with mysteries to be revealed.
And we will lie as volleys of elation will mix and there will be a new creation.
    There will be unity and beauty and mirth; there will be joy and hope and birth.
And your heart and mine will forever entwine.
    Then we will tenderly embrace under a canopy of God's Grace.

THE WILL OF KOHELET

Vanity of Vanities said Kohelet. All is vanity and futile. What gain is there for one's efforts 'neath the sun? Eccl I, 1–3.

Kohelet stood before The Supreme Judge Who Was Considering his fate.
 "Identify yourself, preacher!" Bade The Voice.
"I am Ecclesiastes of the Davidic line who reigned in Zion."
 "Why mention your lineage?
Does it qualify you for some special treatment?" Asked The Voice.

As an arrogant, omniscient sovereign he believed it was his due;
 As a modest mortal of fleeting morality it was not that he knew.
Torn between the two termini Kohelet was silent, evidence of his wisdom.
 "What, preacher, is your legacy to humanity?" Inquired The Voice.

Kohelet took a deep breath, knowing he was on the threshold of death.
 "To the future generations I will be a North Star to guide it in the navigating
Of the repetitive rhythm of life, fruitless as it is."
 Know ye, children to come, that there is a cycle to life
Like the ebb and flow of the tides.
 Each event has its own phase; each period has its own moment.

A time to sow and a time to reap. A time to wound and a time to heal.
 A time to destroy and a time to build.
  A time to mourn and a time to laugh.
A time to lose and a time to find. A time to cast away and a time to gather.
 A time to be distant and a time to be close.
  A time to tear and a time to mend.
A time to speak and a time to be silent. A time to hate and a time to love.
 A time for war and a time for peace.
  A time to begin and a time to end.

But between the apogee and perigee lies a vast ocean of ambiguity.
    The cup of life is filled with emptiness.
        The noble purposes in the heart are meaningless.
            The mind seeking knowledge gathers ignorance.
                The soul filled with charity is self serving.

Generations to come! Futile is it to fathom the Divine Design!
    Your mission is to prove me right or wrong!
The Supreme Judge Contemplated the words of Kohelet and Granted them immortality.

A CODICIL TO THE WILL OF KOHELET

The book of Kohelet is recited on the Sabbath of Succoth, Tabernacles, a pilgrimage festival, during which one Pentateuch cycle ends and another begins. The text deals with cycles in Nature and in human society, a season for every phase of life. Eccl, I-III is the legacy of Kohelet This codicil augments that will.

Oh ye generations to come, Succoth pilgrims in search of sacred
    knowledge,
    I have learned about life through much pain and abundant joy.
From my adventures I have culled wisdom which I will to you.
    Too much reflection invites imperfection;
The soul that is unduly scrutinized becomes unraveled.
    Still study the waxing and waning of the moon!
Know that all human endeavors, likewise, have recurrent phases:
    A time to think, a time to feel; a time to vent emotions,
        a time to hold back;
        A time to work, a time to rest; a time to eat, a time to fast;
        A time to learn, a time to teach; a time to err, a time to repent;
        A time to reproach, a time to forgive; a time to be spirited,
            a time to meditate;
        A time to be gregarious, a time to be alone; a time to take risks,
            a time to be cautious;
        A time to win, a time to lose; a time to add, a time to decrease;
        A time to unite, a time to separate; a time to wander,
            a time to return;
        A time to be jovial, a time to be serious; a time to conform,
            a time to diverge;
        A time to believe, a time to challenge; a time to remember,
            a time to forget;
        A time to etch in memory, a time to overlook; a time to speak,
            a time to be silent.
With a stilled tongue, witnessed by all generations to come,
    I am Kohelet of the sovereign Davidic line.

Poems based on Two Other Holiday Scrolls

TISH'A B'AV

Ninth of Av 586 B.C.E.: When the First Temple was Destroyed

How forlorn lies Zion, Once full of people! Once exalted by the nations, now she is like a widow; her noblest of cities have fallen into bondage. All night long she cries; tears run down her cheek. Zion's people are forsaken and slaves. From the scroll of Lamentations recited in Summer on the 9th day of the Hebrew Calendar. Lam, I, 1-2.

The sun was swallowed by a cloud of pink and disappeared before the eye could blink.
> Darkness reigned; shadows faded when concealed Chaldeans from hills invaded

The city of Zion slashing and burning Judah's lion.
> Skulking like jackals on the prowl at midnight the Chaldeans began to yowl

And rushed away from their makeshift camps and sent up flares from lighted lamps.
> They sped down hills wantonly and fast and set forests on fire, thick and vast.

Night skies blazed; houses were razed.
> The fires spread and thousands were dead.

Orphaned were children; widowed were wives.
> Innocent babies lost their lives.
> Like fire ants the Chaldeans sprinted to The Temple gates.

The sleeping priests knew not what ruin awaits.
> Into the Temple in waves they rolled and stole its copper, bronze, silver, and gold.

The Holy of Holies was willfully defaced and God's Dwelling Place, defiantly disgraced.
> Beheaded priests were strewn in piles, victims of vicious Chaldean wiles.

Holy men burned with patricians in pyres and The Temple was consumed by angry fires.

The stench of death was all about, felling the impious as well as the devout.

Valiant Judeans were trapped and enchained and the blood of freedom from each was drained.

Toward Babylon they were forced to trek, the yoke of captivity upon each neck,

Looking back The Temple they saw, once hallowed ground and cloaked in awe,

Now smoldering in sanguine, fiery ashes capriciously sizzling in frightening flashes.

And when Babylon's waters were reached all sat and wept, and God beseeched.

"Do not despair," was heard in Reply
"The dream of Zion will never die."

NINTH OF AV 586 B.C.E.: A DAY TO FAST

The sea of sky had lost its hue,
    Fading away was its curtain of blue.
Twilight was spreading its shades of black;
    Then trumpets in the hills called to attack.

The Chaldeans hiding in their makeshift camps
    Sent up flares and lighted lamps.
Startled jackals began to stir,
    Moonlight glowed on their golden fur.

How they howled at the waxing night
    And hoarsely barked at all in sight.
Choking on the putrid jackal scent;
    Soldiers jolted in rocky descent.
They slid down the hills clumsy and fast;
    The farmers below were all aghast .
One soldier fell. His broken lamp blazed
    Groves of trees then houses razed.

Like fire ants they swarmed toward each city gate
    Ready to infiltrate.
Through the Temple doors they rolled
    And stole copper, bronze, silver, and gold.

Soldiers entering the Temple treasury
    Beheaded priests with sadistic savagery.
The Holy of Holies was recklessly defaced
    And God's dwelling place wantonly disgraced.

The sacrificial altar was desecrated,
    Destruction continued unabated.
An arriving flank rammed the hewn stone foundation;
    Relentless was the devastation.

Another flank brandished adze and axe
    And splintered palm trees with countless whacks.
And another torched the olive wood doors
    And yet another, the cedar wood floors.

Yesterday's Temple had grace and style
    Today's is rubble and a smoking pile .
Flames licked here and flames licked there;
    The city of dreams was now a nightmare.

Streaming out gasping for breath,
    Afraid their soot filled lungs would hasten death
Were terrified Judeans: rich and poor;
    The simple in tastes and the epicure;

The young, the old; the coward, the bold;
    The humble, the arrogant; the righteous, the insolent;
The pious priest, the lyric Levite;
    The scheming sinner, the sincerely contrite.

Dodging soldiers bent on cremating,
    They ran to gates where lancers were waiting
Like howling wolves pouncing on prey.
    There was no hope, there was only dismay.

For Zion's Children were damned without any trial and started for Babylon and into exile.
    A scrim of dust, soot, sorrow, and ash descended on Zion, now a heap of trash.
The hobbling captives heard the crying of burning sheep who in fields lay dying.
    Forlorn and melancholy filled, witnesses to the blood that had been spilled

They inched along in funeral procession grieving their loss and dispossession
> From the land, God Promised gem, a flawless jewel in The Divine Diadem.

Shoulders Stooped with trembling legs they were rushed and prodded and called "dregs of dregs,"
> Opening a chapter of history in Babylonian captivity.

* * * * *

The Levites with voices fine sang their story line by line,
> Wailing the age-old litany: the marrow of vanity is vanity.

We have lied, we have cheated. we were proud and conceited.
> We blasphemed and extorted and God's Words distorted.

We coveted what our neighbors had
> And acted on the Sabbath what The Law forbade.

Our offerings to God were lacking in zeal;
> We ignored the ordeal of the sick and of the poor.

And to the lowly we were unjust;
> We forgot how to love, knew only to lust.

We had doubted the words of the prophet of doom
> Who shouted his thoughts and heightened our gloom.

"A thousand years of history have gone up in flame
> But do we alone deserve the blame?"

Volleys of anger rolled off Isaiah's tongue;
> Vexation and rage tuned the songs he had sung,
>> "What about the marauding Chaldeans.
>> Are they more virtuous than the plundered Judeans?
>> How can the Babylonians be paragons of learning,
>> When what they do best is looting and burning?
>> Where were You God, Shield of the oppressed?
>> And where was Zion's valiant Heaven Blessed?
>> No one aided us in our plight
>> No one comforted us in our fright."

* * * * *

The captives were alone, dismayed, and dejected
    And from their Maker disconnected.
Their spirits were desolate and flowed with ennui,
    Languor, aimlessness, and anomie.
Passing caravans sneered at their condition
    And arrogantly ridiculed their indisposition.

* * * * *

Meanwhile, they were unwashed and underfed,
    Fleas and lice crawled on each head,
And relentless sun beat upon their skins
    As their tormented souls recalled their sins.
When they reached Babylon's flowing waters
    They wept for Zion's sons and daughters
And lamented the loss of their spiritual mother,
    The Holy City, now ruled by another.
They yearned, they pined and cursed the thief
    Who stole Zion's life and filled them with grief.

They washed in river and drank from stream and dedicated themselves
    to rebuild their dream.

> "Wisps of mortals have we become,
> Hungry, unclean and spiritually numb.
> Petulant and arrogant we've been in the past
> But to beg Your Forgiveness today we fast."

To their previous foibles they contritely admitted
    And to God's Sacred Covenant they recommitted.
"Cleanse us, O Lord, of our guilt and our shame,
    "Do it," they prayed, "in Thy Holy Name!
"Refill our lamp, rekindle our light;
    Let the beacon to all nations again shine bright."

Day after day they repeated their plea,
> Reminding themselves that God once Set them free
From Egypt where they had been slaves
> And then in the desert spared them from graves.
The Children of Zion, becoming chaste and pure,
> From their adversity God had rendered a cure.
Raveling their hope, conversion was planted
> And the redemption of Zion was mercifully granted.
To God, the Source of life's inspiration,
> They pledged eternal consecration.
No longer in terror, no longer afraid,
> Bowing their heads, they fervently prayed.
"To Thy Great Name holiness bestow."
> And the Angels on high Answered "Let it be so."

ESTHER, THE HEROINE

Scholars are of several opinions regarding the Book of Esther, the main characters of which are Esther, Mordecai, Ahasueros, and Haman. Some view the story as pure allegory; others as true history. Scholars disagree as to the identity of Ahasueros. Some say it was Xerxes who reigned from 486–465 B.C. Others say it was Artaxerxes who reigned from 405- 359 B.C. It is likely that the text has been edited several times and what remains is a tale of Jewish heroism. God's Name is not found in the text. Furthermore, no Book of Esther was found in the library at Qumrum. Nevertheless the story is an integral part of Judeo-Christian lore. The book is read on the holiday of Purim, Feast of Lots, a day of complete merriment, and perhaps, abandonment.

It came to pass in the reign of Ahasueros who ruled from India to Ethiopia. In the third year of his reign he made a banquet attended by nobles, princes and his servants, the powers of Persia and Media. Vashti, his queen, made a feast for the women in the royal house. With a merry heart he ordered Vashti to come into his presence and show his guests her beauty. She refused to comply. His advisors urged him to banish her otherwise when word got out all of the wives in his kingdom would disobey their husbands. He agreed. After she was banished, Ahasueros looked for a replacement. Esther was brought before the king and she pleased him. Esth I, 3- II-9.

Each Purim a tale's retold of a drunken king in Persia of old.
    He commanded his wife to entertain his tipsy friends. But his demands were all in vain.
She stretched out on her royal bed and this is what she firmly said,
    "King! I will not charm your fellow drunks!" He said, "Vashti! Pack your trunks!"
The king awoke next day at dawn; now sober found Vashti was gone.
    His drinking had been so much fun, he could not remember what wrong he had done.
All alone and feeling blue, he asked his advisors what he now should do.
    "Find a wife who is well bred, she'll restore your life when next you wed.

"Find me a wife," he, then, decreed.
    His aides left the palace at utmost speed.
Combing the land for a damsel fair,
    they discovered one of beauty quite rare
    With sparkling eyes and golden hair.
    She was a star and answered to ESTAIR.
Well the king and EsTAIR did not tarry and at once set out to marry.

One day ESTAIR began to cry. She missed her cousin Mordecai.
    "Send for him," commanded The Crown and apparel him in ministerial gown.
Mordecai became the king's advisor and in all of Persia there was never one wiser.

Haman, though, the thought had savored that *he* was the wise man the king had favored.
    For some reason, we know not why, Haman decided all the Hebrews must die.
So this very wily man set upon a uncalled-for plan.
    He built gallows where Hebrews would swing.
        This would surely amuse the king.
But Haman's plan did not please Mordecai who did not think the Jews should die.
    Mordecai told ESTAIR of Haman's plan. She then asked the king Haman's plan to ban.
If Haman hangs every Hebrew, EsTAIR pleaded then she'd hang, too.
    The Hebrews would be an endangered species if Haman his way had with his evil theses.
But that is not how this story ended; the king had human rights defended.
    He declared that the hateful Haman, instead, will wear a noose around his head.
Some tales have endings that are gory. That is true of this story.
    Still there's a moral for every gang who dreams of evil:
    you will surely hang.

Other Writings

GOLDEN SAYINGS OF SOLOMON FOR HIS DAY AND SINCE

The proverbs of Solomon, son of David, king of Israel teach wisdom and discretion, confidence, poise, and ways to succeed. The pure will be endowed with shrewdness; the young with foresight. Regarding God in awe is the beginning of wisdom. based on Prov I-VIII.

Solomon gathered scholars of all generations: past, present, and future
    To teach them what he had learned from *his* life.
The scholars charted his teachings for their students
    And their students refashioned them for their generations.
These are the golden words that glistened like pearls upon Solomon's tongue;
    These are the splendid thoughts that sparkled like sunlight upon Solomon's lips,
Listen to my words with a keen ear, he said;
    Hearken to my thoughts with a discerning heart, he declared.
Sow the seeds of Wisdom by revering God:
    Root of Intelligence, Source of Prudence, Fount of Reason.
Wisdom Calls to all in the streets and in the market place,
    Sapience Summons all at the city gates:
The young, the old; the wise, the dolt; the sage, the oaf;
    Wisdom Speaks to fathers and mothers and to sisters and brothers;
Sapience Speaks to teachers and students, to rulers and subjects.
    Let these sayings be your guide; let these precepts be your beacon.
    At all times under all circumstances.
        Love knowledge; neither flout nor flaunt learning;
Confess humbly your ignorance; be modest in your show of knowledge.
        Be honest, just, and fair; be loyal and faithful;
            Scorn evil; speak Truth;
          Plan carefully; prepare diligently;
           Be calm; vanquish inner tumult;

Cherish your loved ones; treasure your friends;
Be ambitious; shun indolence:
Value virtue; never cheat;
Learn from rebuke; flourish by approval;
Be strong in a crisis:be clear-head in an emergency;
Hold your wrath:radiate your delight;
Revile no one's name; praise the efforts of others;
Seek candor; shun deceit;
Do not lament your failures; accept your flaws;
Do not rejoice when others stumble; be a comfort to those who fumble;
Do not be vexed at the insolent; appreciate the courteous;
Be solemn in your grief,be happy in your mirth;
Envy not; do not carry a grudge;
Correct children when they err; praise children when they try;
Never abandon hope; have faith in yourself and in others;
Love builds; hate destroys;
Drain yourself of malice; fill your soul with charity;
Do not gloat over your wealth; do not boast about your difficulties;
Tend to the sick; feed the hungry;
Clothe the unclad; shelter the homeless;
Share your happiness with others; reveal your bitterness to no one;
Worry pillages energy; serenity restores the soul;
Gloom is no companion; woe is no friend;
Respect what the elderly knows; value what the young teaches;
Favor not the rich; advocate for the poor;
Do not exploit the helpless; do not pander to the rich;
Hold all to a high standard of merit; gauge all with the same yardstick.

SOLOMON'S EPILOGUE

In wending your way through life and in embarking on your voyage to maturity
> Do not wear yourself out pursuing wealth;
>> do not exhaust yourself amassing prestige.

Do not shackle yourself to your misery but undo the chains that fetter your laughter.
> Always put your faith in The Creator; ever trust in God.

Be exact in your gauges; be precise in your rules.
> Avoid quick schemes; be not lured by false promises.

No matter the circumstances you will endure;
> No matter the adversity, you will survive.

Direct your steps in the path of light;
> detour from the path of darkness.
>> Wisdom Hates pride and arrogance;
>>> Sapience Deplores smugness and deceit.
>> Wisdom Favors builders; Sapience Sustains conservers.
>> Wisdom Brings happiness; Sapience Brings joy.

Thank God daily for your Blessings; thank God for your wisdom.
> Pray with a sincere heart; call on God with reverence
>> And you will reap Wisdom; and you will harvest Sapience.

> Remember these sayings, too. Do not forget these maxims.

A CHRONICLE WRITTEN ON THE TEMPLE WALL IN TWO VOICES[1]

Wall: Today I am an age´d wall, crumbling here and there, wailing, crying true tears,
   Remembering what once was. The last to see the rays of the sun at the close of day,
   I saw more of history than the other walls combined.
   In the olden days I buttressed The Holy Temple.
   Supporting the other walls, sustaining Zion despite its impure sacrifices
   Penetrating the pores of my stones and decorating them with decay.
   I started to deteriorate, not so much from a chemical reaction
   But from the weight of Zion's sins.
   First, it was Solomon himself. The "wise one." The "pious one."
   He built an altar to a pagan god to please one of his all too many alien wives.
   Then his son, Rehoboam further defiled the Temple and sinned against You, God.
   After repenting, You, God of Compassion, Forgave him. Still the stench of sin remained.
   His son Abijah succeeded him and added his sin to those of his fathers.
   But his son, Asa, abolished pagan worship and purified the Temple.
   Merciful God! You Looked favorably upon him.

Psalmist: *Blessed are they who walk not in the counsel of the sinners*
   Nor stand in the way of the sinners.

Wall: But the seeds of cruelty sown by his father sprouted in his declining days

---

1. The first voice is that of 'The Wall" the second voice, in *italics*, is that of the poet who wrote Psalm I. *Like Deuteronomy in the Pentateuch, The Books of Chronicles chiefly summarizes Israelite history during the monarchy. The editor, however, does not always stick to the material in the books of Samuel and of Kings. The era described is also one in which the prophets were Called to reform the people.*

> And once again sin was added to sin. It drained my core of its essence.
> When he was gathered to his ancestors, Jehoshafat, his son, was crowned king.
> He did what was good in Your Eyes.

Psalmist: *Blessed are they whose delight is in the Lord.*

Wall: Then his son, Jehoram, was crowned king.
Having killed his own brothers,
He married the daughter of Ahab, King of Israel, Your enemy and enemy of Judah.
He built pagan altars; worshipped idols; removed priests from their sacred duties.

Psalmist: *The wicked are like the chaff which the wind drives away.*

Wall: No one lamented his death when it came;
no one recited psalms.
Ahaziah, his son, ruled, less than a year.
Like father, like son, another layer of sin darkened my face.
His mother reigned next. She was no better.
After her passing, Joash ruled.
He smashed idols and cleansed the Temple.
But a skulking evil spirit showed its face
And he killed the high priest, in the Temple courtyard.
In the courtyard no less!
His hypocrite son, Amaziah, continued the cleansing but died in a war with his cousins in Israel.
Then his son, Uzziah, acted righteously and You, Adonai, Renewed the Temple.
But toward the end of his days he became arrogant and subordinated the priests to him.
You Gave him a skin disease, making him ritually unclean. His son, Jotham, came next.
He walked in the ways of Moses, The Law giver.

Psalmist: *Blessed are they who meditate day and night on the Law of the Lord.*

Wall: But his son, Ahaz, did not. Ahaz even sacrificed his own sons on a metal altar to Baal.
    Gravely his sins weigh on me yet, my mortar decays.
But his son, Hezekiah, purified the Temple and rededicated it and straight did I stand.
    Although the sins of his fathers had eroded my core, I felt renewed, ritually clean, standing proudly to honor You, Author of the Universe.

Psalmist: *The leaf of the righteous does not wither.*

Wall: But his son, Manasseh, rebuilt the places of pagan worship and sacrificed his own sons
    As had his grandfather, Ahaz. My innards began to crumble.
I watched him chained and manacled and dragged off to Babylon.

Psalmist: *Sinners do not stand in the congregation of the righteous.*

Wall: He repented his sins and You, Font of Mercy, Forgave him.
    Upon his return to Jerusalem he repaired Your altar.

Psalmist: *The Lord knows the ways of the righteous.*

Wall: But his son, Amon, sinned against You and did not repent.
    I watched his advisors assassinate him.
Imagine a son of Zion taking the life of another son of Zion.
    It was not the first time I witnessed this
And it was not to be the last.

Psalmist: *The ways of the sinner shall perish.*

Wall: His son, Josiah, strictly obeyed the laws of Moses. I heard him read the Book of the Covenant.
    His voice was penitent and sincere. His melodies so stirred me that I trembled with awe.

Psalmist: *The righteous bring forth their fruit in the proper season.*

Wall: He died in battle, though, and Jeremiah composed a lament for him.

    Joahaz was next in the Davidic line.

But his brother Jehoyakim, favored by the king of Egypt, replaced him.

    More sin. More blot on the history of Zion. More fungus growing on my face.

Nebuchadnezzar dragged him in chains to Babylon.

His son, Jehoyachin, ruled three months.

    In that time he defiled the Temple more than any of his predecessors.

His uncle Zedekiah ruled by the appointment of Nebuchadnezzar.

    When he allowed the Babylonian tyrants to slaughter Zion's youth in the Temple

The upper layer of my stony face toppled from the weight of such sin.

    The soul of Zion hemorrhaged and was not stanched.

My cracks are filled with shame because he spoke ill of Jeremiah, the sainted prophet.

    The other walls of the Temple were torched by the Babylonian aggressors and fell.

I, injured, an old wall, weakened here and there, heavy with tears,

    Charred with ashes of memory, still remain upright, a reminder of Zion's wayward ways

But also a hopeful model that spirits can be cleansed and Zion can be reborn into righteousness.

    On that day all creation will walk in Your Path, bringing You joy and granting You peace.

THREE PSALMS

Happy are they who reject the counsel of the wicked, who do not follow the model of sinners, or join those who reject God. Instead, they delight in God's Teachings and study daily. Ps, I, 1.

Blesse´d are they with joy who walking through life
    Scorn the cheat,
      Shun the sinner,
        And ignore the mocker.
Day and night they are Praised
    Who with ardor, faith, and resolve study God's Scriptures
      Which are like the roots of fruit trees nourished and sustained
In deep-reaching, fertile ancient streams, and throughout Time renew
    themselves and blossom.
        God Guides the pure in heart but Turns Away from evil
    doers.

The Lord is my Shepherd I shall not want. He makes me lie down in green pastures, He leads me by still waters, He Guides me in right paths. He is my strength. Ps, 23, 1–3.

O God! Ever my Comfort and my Guide!
    Lacking nothing, I, a humble piece of clay,
Unafraid, lie with Your Blesséd Sons and Daughters
    By green pastures beside calm waters.
With Mercy You Show me the Right Path to walk;
    With Kindness You Return me to Your Flock.
I am not concerned about what is sure to come;
    What mortal can ever Death's darkness plumb?
But restored am I by Your Love Divine
    And ever will I dwell in Your Sacred Shrine.

      O God! You Restore my soul and Give Solace to all.

All the earth shout for God; worship God in gladness; go before before Him with joy. Ps 100, 1.

All dwellers on earth
    Worship together with joy.
Praise the One and Only God.
    Kindle the Sacred Flame;
Bless God's Holy Name.
    O God! Fount of Mercy.
Your Truth Endures forever.

All nations join together to offer thanks to God.

RENEWAL IN THE DAYS OF EZRA AND NEHEMIA

We, the people of Israel, the priests, the Levites, the Temple guards, the Temple musicians, the workmen, and all others who obey God's Word have separated from the foreigners living in our land, we, our wives and children join with our leaders to live by God's Laws. We will not intermarry with the strangers in our land. Neh X, 28–30.

Memory, in tatters, was swallowed by the abyss of Time
    Where the spark of Sinai, smothered by indifference, drifted into extinction.
Then there gathered in Jerusalem the exiles who had returned:
    Priests, gate keepers, singers, temple servants, persons of distinction
Husbands and "wives and all their sons and daughters."
    In God's Eyes each one the same as another in wisdom; each equal to the other.
All with one purpose: to hear the Levites read from the scroll of the Law
    That God had Given to Moses. At that moment of bonding,
They rededicated themselves to God; at that moment they again became God's people.
    Then did the sun peering through history rekindle the lamp that guided their ancestors
Through the bleakness of the past.
    And they passed it on for untold generations to come.

EZRA

Jewish men were choosing foreign women as brides; and so God's holy people became defiled. The leaders were the main wrongdoers. Ezra IX, 2

When Ezra, the priest, to Zion returned, his eyes wept when he learned
    That many Hebrew bridegrooms did foreign wives choose.
Assimilation corrodes the marrow of our souls and with pomp extols
    What is vile and does our God defile.
He gathered the people at The Temple gate
    And bid the men to send back any mate
Who false gods accepts and lives not by the precepts
    Of the Mosaic creed as God Had Decreed.
That day saddened brides cried in shame for each had lost her marriage name.
    Ezra believed that strangers impure would be an overture
To extinction of the race and in time Jews would disappear without a trace.
    The people hailed Ezra, the wise; never would he his faith compromise.
There was a Hebrew, though, who loved his wife so that he did not agree to let her go.
    And the people threw stones at his head until life left his body and he fell down dead.

THE LEGEND OF JONAH (C 760 B.C.)

God's Words came to Jonah. Go at once to Nineveh and publish judgment against it for I Learned of their evil doing. However, Jonah fled from Joppa and boarded a ship to Tarshish ignoring God's Request. But God Sent a mighty wind upon the sea and the ship was in danger of collapsing. Jonah I, 1–4.

Jonah heard a Voice saying Nineveh is a city of sin.
    Go there and cleanse the wickedness they spin.
Jonah feared he heard the Voice of God and ran the other way.
    Who was he, Jonah, to tell the people that they had gone astray.
While on a boat headed for Spain
    There arose dark clouds bursting with rain.
His boat rocked and rolled;
    The captain its steering no longer controlled.
"Pray to your gods this tempest to stop."
    As each sailor's stomach was going flip flop.
Jonah who was hiding in the hold of the boat
    Said he was to blame for loss of the float.
He jumped into the water so the storm would subside
    And once again the sea returned to the normal tide.
A fish Sent by God was there awaiting
    As the raging waters began abating.
Jonah felt his heavy heart thumping;
    Jonah felt his skin was jumping.
The gigantic fish a safe haven provided
    For the prophet Jonah, who had been misguided.
He cried In his profound distress, "O God to You my thanks I profess
    For saving my life of so little worth among the many righteous here on earth."
God Surrounded Jonah with Heavenly Grace Which Jonah's soul did warmly Embrace.
    In three days, not one day more,
The fish disgorged Jonah and sent him to shore.
    Immediately did he to Nineveh go with the Grace of God was he all Aglow.

God's Message he gave with a silver tongue and the penitent people around him clung.
    Deeply they lamented the wrongs they had done and lifted themselves from oblivion.
And God's Heart was Filled with Pity Sublime Pity for Nineveh city teaming with crime.
    But Jonah complained these people possessed a venal trait;
And should punishment not pity be their deserving fate?
    But Jonah learned that God Acquits
The wayward who wrongful acts commits.

JERUSALEM, THE NEW

The king ordered his minister to choose from the Israelite exiles young men of the royal family and of the noble families who were handsome, intelligent, and free from physical defects to serve in the royal court. Among those chosen was Daniel. Dan I, 3-6.

Nebuchadnezzar, Babylon's king, had a dream, a troublesome dream.
    It made him scream.
No minister could explain the frightful dream.
    No minister could decipher the theme.
Daniel, with Merciful God's Guidance, explained
    The king's dream and maintained
That God Showed him the way
    The dream's meaning to convey.
Daniel addressed the king
    Who with his friends swigging .
"Before you was a giant statue, shining and bright.
    Head of gold; the chest and arms were silver like moonlight.
Bronze was its waste.
    Then a stone from a cliff broke loose and the statue defaced.
All at once the metals crumbled to dust and a wind carried it hence.
    There was no defense
Against the force.
    There was no recourse."
Your empire will crumble no matter how solidly it was grounded.
    No matter how firmly it was founded.
There will be no way to unite Babylon with any other state.
    There will be no way new empires to placate.
Babylon is doomed,
    Once flourishing will soon be consumed."
Nebuchadnezzar was distraught but accepted the fact.
    Babylon would be attacked.
Nebuchadnezzar, impressed, presented Daniel with gifts galore
    And told him that he would Zion restore.
Daniel gave thanks to God for his revelation
    For what would happen to this once mighty nation.

THE FUTURE OF JERUSALEM

Through your keen-sighted eyes, Daniel, I can now see Jerusalem
    A newborn crawling out of an ancient womb
Bearing crosses, crescents, and stars of David up the sacred mounts
    And beating them into plowshares.

RETURN FROM EXILE

In the first year of Cyrus king of Persia God Inspired the heart of Cyrus king of Persia to declare throughout his realm: God of Heaven, Has Made me responsible to build a temple for him at Jerusalem in Judah. Anyone of God's people may go there. II Chr 22-23.

Cyrus

Day after day the Judean exiles filled the waters of Babylon with their tears.
    "O God," they keened," send us a redeemer. We have suffered for so many years.
Orphans are we and widows, too; in sackcloth we dress.
    We smear our faces with ashes and our sins daily confess."
Although exile purified their souls and every sin they did repent,
    Angered over their iniquities, God did not yet Relent.
"Our souls are no longer black; to the Torah we adhere."
    And, in time, God saw that their atonement was sincere.
In Persia there was a king who embodied all that was right
    And was inspired to conquer Babylon, civilization's blight.
Koresh[2] was his name
    And for purity[3] was he known.
With his army of Persian soldiers the Babylonians were overthrown.
    "Children of Israel," he wrote, "return home rededicated
And rebuild your Holy House which to God was consecrated."
    And he gave back the cattle, the silver and the gold,
As well as the sacred relics the Babylonians stole.
    And the Israelites learned a lesson: a righteous life to lead
And were grateful to the Persian savior who from bondage had them freed.
    And God Learned a lesson, too. Vengeful not to be;
But to accept human imperfections and to the repentant Grant amnesty.

---

2. Cyrus
3. Kosher, pure, an anagram of Koresh.

The Return

The Judeans into exile went and had many years to mourn and to lament
    Strangers took over their Jerusalem homes and busily built colonies in honeycombs.
The strangers' children, knowing nothing of the past, thought their ownership would always last.
    And the first Judeans who from exile returned were by the strangers cursed and spurned.
Although the strangers resisted the returnees insisted,
    "We have permission from the Persian king to reclaim everything
We lost when we were dragged into exile by the Assyrians, base and vile."
    The strangers said the Jews had no rights. And scuffled with them in violent fights.
But alas the Persian kings decreed that Jews who from captivity had been freed
    Were the rightful owners of the land given to them by God's Command.
Strangers and Jews lived side by side, both arguing their claims were justified.

JOB'S SUIT

Heavenly creatures gathered about God, Satan among them. What have you been doing, Asked God. "Wandering around the Earth," Satan replied. "Did you see My servant, Job?" Asked God. "He is faithful and exalts Me and is heedful not to commit a wrong." Satan replied "would he still exalt You if he got nothing out of it? Now suppose you take everything away from him would he curse You?" God Said, "I will Agree to your scheme just don't hurt him." Job I, 6–12.

Satan, advocate of evil, spoke to God, saying, Job, your holiest of men,
    Would blaspheme Your Name if You had not Rewarded him with riches.
"Let me take away his health, his wealth, and his children
    And See if he *still* Exalts you."
God Doubted that Job would change,
    So righteous was he.
In a blink of an eye Job lost his health, his wealth, and several children.
    It was like a tornado ripped through his soul,
Rending his spirit and destroying his mooring.
    How much more hardship would he be enduring.?
"Why me, Merciful God,? Why me, "he pleaded,
    "What have I done to deserve my fate?
    Was I some kind of rogue? Some kind of cheat?
Did I engage in deceit? Did I my neighbor mistreat?
    What sin have I committed to be so punished?
    Yesterday I had ten children;
Yesterday I had fertile land, sheep, and wealth.
    Yesterday the poor begged alms of me;
    Yesterday I was of good cheer; yesterday my skin was clear.
Yesterday the priests sought my counsel.
    Yesterday I had an adoring wife.
    Yesterday I had a good life.
Yesterday I had everything; today I have nothing.
    Not a thing. Nothing! Nothing but festering wounds.
Did I not make proper sacrifices to You in the name of my forgetful children?

> Did I not make proper sacrifices of thanks to You for the bounty Your Gave me?
>
> Today my children are dead. My three daughters were defiled.
>> Today the winds dried my fields; today the marauding Chaldeans burned them,
>
> Stole my sheep, and destroyed my house.
>> Today my skin is diseased and I am distressed.
>
> Yesterday I was Blessed; today I am Cursed.
>> Today the poor scoff at me and the priests scorn me.
>
> Where can I now find shelter? How can I now earn a living?
>> What I have been taught and what I learned well
>
> Is that the good sow kindness and reap righteousness;
>> And the righteous plant piety and harvest grace.
>
> Merciful God Does not Punish the innocent; Compassionate God Does not Flog the virtuous.
>> My wife says, "Denounce God"!
>> My wife says, "Curse The Creator."
>
> Because I have lost all, my friends say, I have faltered;
>> Because I have been so humbled, my comrades say, I have sinned.
>
> My woes, they say, grew from my iniquities; my wounds, they say, are due to my sins.
>> But when have I committed an iniquity? But how have I sinned?
>
> Merciful God, You Fill my dreams with terror.
>> Compassionate Creator, You Torment my soul.
>> Who will condole me? My friends? No. You God? No.
>
> Why have You Dismissed me like a nobody?
>> Why have You Robbed me of being a somebody?
>> Is sorrow to be my legacy? Is pain to be my heritage?
>
> Friends say doubt not the Merciful God; comrades say question not the compassionate Creator.
>> What comfort have they given me?
>> What consolation do they offer?
>
> I am equal to them in wisdom: they speak cliches, folklore, and ignorance.
>> Did You God Appoint them my prosecutors?
>> Did You God Name them my accusers?
>
> My friends have abandoned me! You Have Deserted me.

> Who will now defend me? Who but myself will be my advocate?
I am all alone: my dreams are windblown.
> Can You God Explain my misery?
>> Can You God Unravel my torment?
Do my angry words flow from my affliction?
>> Does my rage grow from my misfortune?
> Hear my voice, O Merciful God!
>> Listen to my words, O Compassionate Creator.
Do not Destroy my hope; Do not demolish my faith.
> Have I condemned You for *Your* Blunders? |
>> Have I blamed You for *Your* Mistakes?
Job's mind was reeling in turmoil;
> Love and hate melded with regret and defeat.
Job's soul was raw and anguished
> Yet yoked with adoration for God once cherished.
Then a Voice Came through the storm; mournful words Sprung from the sea of sorrows.
> Job your pain is My pain, too. Job your distress is Mine also.
Survival means struggle; life is filled with trials.
> Question Me! Doubt Me!
But never give up the struggle. Never surrender !
> Never give up hope in human goodness, My Gift to mortals.
And Job knew that God Is near and not aloof;
> And Job knew that God is beyond reproof.
And Job knew that God Does Not control fate
> And Job knew that God Does not Ordain, Control, or Dictate.
Satan was defeated and left his heavenly abode;
> He lost the standing God Had Bestowed.
On his journey to the bowels of the earth
> He melted into chaos and was without worth.

4 The Apocrypha

The word "Apocrypha" is from the Greek. It means "hidden." But what precisely "hidden" means is open to question. To some it means esoteric; to others, disputed? to others of less value than the authentic books of the Bible? The Apocrypha consists of books that are not in the Jewish canon or many Protestant canons. It became part of the Catholic canon in 1546 at the Council of Trent and is regarded as part of the Bible by the Anglican Communion. These faiths regard the texts as "revealed." However, neither Philo not Josephus, both historians, make mention of apocryphal works. Topics in the Apocrypha range from prayers (of Manasseh) to valor and heroes (Susannah and Tobit), to moral behavior (ben Sirach). Although these works are not viewed as "sacred or Inspired" they illustrate religious literary works from a Hellenic period of Jewish history

THE PSALM OF MANASSEH

God of Abraham, Isaac, and Jacob and their righteous children. I am a sinner: for I have transgressed beyond the number of the sands of the sea. I am not worthy to see the height of heaven for the multitude of my evils. I am bowed down with many iron bands, that I cannot lift up mine head, neither have any release: for I have provoked Your Wrath. I did not do Your Will, neither kept I Your Commandments: I have set up abominations. Therefore I bow the knee of mine heart, beseeching Your Grace. I have sinned, O Lord, I have sinned, and I confess my iniquities: humbly I beseech You to Forgive me. Pr Man, 1-14.

Blessed is the True Judge,
    God of Abraham, Isaac, and Jacob.
I hold a mirror to my soul.
    I, Manasseh, had forgotten

I had forgotten the True Judge
> I had forgotten those I sentenced to death,
>> Including my saintly grandfather, the great prophet, Isaiah,
>>> And infants sacrificed alive to the do-nothing, stone god, Baal.

I stand before you confessing my transgressions.
> I stand before you in deep sorrow for the suffering I have caused.
>> I stand before you in abject remorse.
>>> I cannot undo what damage I have done to my people
>>>> I cannot undo what harm, injury and agony I have wrought.
>>>>> I cannot right the wrongs I have committed.

I am a sullied, stained, defiled stem of the stalk of David
> I reek of sin. I strayed from Your Ways
>> My soul is infected and decaying.

Can You Show Mercy to me who imposed forced labor?
> I feel the weight of the stones and lumber I made my people carry to build a palace.

I have wronged them.
> Their cries, their pain, their suffering drain me of sleep.
>> A thousand times have I repented;
>> A thousand times have I deplored what I had done.

Each day I study Your Laws until They are inscribed on the precincts of my heart
> And housed upon the furrows of my forehead.

They are frontlets between my eyes.
> Humbly do I rest my case.

Angels argued with God not trust his Contrition.
> Others Pleaded with the Merciful God to Show Charity.

God Opened the Gates of Repentance
> And Manasseh was Forgiven as are all sinners who in sorrow sincerely repent.

JUDITH'S VICTORY OVER THE ASSYRIANS

Then King Nebuchadnezzar sent a message to the Persians and surrounding countries to join him in a war against King Arphaxad of the Medes. They ignored him. They thought he had no chance of winning. This threw Nebuchadnezzar into a rage and he vowed to risk his entire kingdom to take revenge against all of those people. Jdt I, 5-12

As the returnees from exile were The Temple rebuilding,
> A menace from the East innocent blood was spilling.

Nebuchadnezzar terrorized nations far and wide
> Over the fertile crescent he sought to preside.

The exiles were weary; their prospects were eerie.
> Into Judah the Assyrians scattered;
>> whomever they saw, they cruelly battered.

Many Judeans hid in the hills; sick with fever they shivered with chills.
> The people moaned; the people groaned for our sins have we not already atoned?

Why are we now in such dire straits;
> why is there no food upon our plates?
>> Is it better to submit and become Assyrian slaves

Or lie as carrion without benefit of graves?
> The people accosted Uzziah, the priest, saying you eat your feast

But we are homeless and without food because of your hostile attitude
> Toward the Assyrians to whom you had not condescended

And now we are a people who Nebuchadnezzar offended.
> Wait my people. I will pray and prod and beg for mercy from The One True God.

If in five days amnesty is not granted then to Assyria we'll be transplanted.
> It is better to live as slaves than to die in battle as weaklings and knaves.

At that time there lived Judith, a widow devout, who sent her servant to search out
> The town officials who she did reprimand because they would surrender the sacred land.

How dare you, she said, put yourselves in God's Place;
>how dare you test God's Grace.

The human is too blind to see into God's Mind.

Our town must not surrender; our town needs a defender.
>The officials were chastened by the widow devout from whose soul virtue did sprout.

Judith's eyes moved from man to man as she said I have a plan.
>Trust me to do it right ask me nothing just give me the night.

To ward off those who were aggressing, the priest gave her his official blessing.
>Judith retreated to the room where she'd pray and asked of God to Show her the way

To use a sword as did Simon of old who avenged the raped Dinah with an action bold.
>The Assyrians are boastful and proud and terrorize Zion like a thundercloud.

Please God Stand by my side as I, a woman, break their pride.
>Their general Holofernes may be wise in war but You, God, are my Counselor.

God Sharpened her mind a strategy to find.
>Her legs did not quail as she put on her veil

And entered Holofernes tent. By the God of Zion had she Been Sent.
>A table of cakes, figs and wine she spread but it was Judith he wanted to lie in his bed.

He drank and drank until he fell asleep then Judith toward him did stealthily creep.
>She unsheathed the sword beneath her dress and across his throat she did it impress.

Calmly she left the general's tent and back to her home she contentedly went.
>When the Assyrians saw Holofernes' lifeless head they quaked and from Zion they sped.

From Jerusalem came the High Priest to honor Judith at a victory feast.
>Before all assembled a blessing he gave to Judith, the widow, who Zion did save.

Long life to you he said again and again and the people responded, "Amen, Amen."

SUSANNAH

Every day at noon when the men left for lunch, Susanah went for a walk in the garden. Two judges were so enthralled by her beauty that they would wait around and watch for her. Each was ashamed to admit their lust. One day they jumped out and said they would like to have sex with her. She refused. Then the judges testified against her and wanted to put her death. Sus I, 7–28.

Her beauty was without compare! How comely was her face;
How elegant was her grace never would she stroll about with an air.
> With deep devotion to God she would pray to send help to those in need,
> To heal the sick with utmost speed, and mourners' anguish to tenderly allay.

Her husband, Joakim, in her had trust but employed two judges, corrupt and depraved
Who swooned when they saw her and craved her body, so filled were they with lust.
> One day they did upon her spy, her servants having left her alone.
> A poisoned envy within them had grown, each craved for the chance with her to lie.

But she refused.
> So that all would shun her they proclaimed her a whore.

They claimed they saw her kiss her amour who had her chemise with his hand undone.
> The people believed the jealous judges foul who condemned Susannah to death.
> With a gasp of her remaining breath she sent out a wailing howl,

"Oh God Who Watches over all that I do Correct this injustice of the judges uncouth
Send a Messenger who will tell the truth and prevent justice from going askew."
> God Implored Daniel, brave and wise, to defend Susanah, righteous and devout,
>> Whose name smeared by judges who spout lies and against her the people to mobilize.

Then came Daniel who proved to the lot that Susanah was faithful, of this he was sure,

She had always been pure and faithful to the laws of Moses as she had been taught.

In their lies the judges had been caught.
    O what misery they had wrought.

So the two judges, tainted and depraved, their sentence to Susannah themselves received

For having the people of Israel deceived.
    And the virtuous Susannah by Daniel was saved.

BARUCH

O Almighty God, our anguished spirits cry out to You. Hear us and have Mercy because we have sinned against You. You Abide ever more but when we die it is Forever. Hear our prayers from dying voices, The sins of our ancestors weigh heavily upon us. Be Forgiving for You Are God, Abundant in Power. Bar III, 1-6.

They were wrenched from their humble abodes in Jerusalem
    And forced to march to Nineveh
In dusty heat that choked their nostrils
    And nightly cold that chilled every bone.

Desolate Children of Zion, donned in black,
    Bereft of their beloved temple
And distressed that their king
    No longer sat on his throne

Sat on the banks of the Tigris
    And wept as they watched flotsam and jetsam
Float down the river.
    They knew they had sinned and sought to atone.

Baruch, scribe to the great prophet Jeremiah,
    First denounced their wayward ways
And then, seeing their remorse was genuine,
    Pleaded with God not to Disown

Zion's melange who 'though once they had strayed
    Now suffer the duress of exile:
The offal in the streets, the abuses by the Babylonians,
    And the weight of a cervical millstone.

"O Eternal One," he pleaded, "we are burdened with guilt,
    Rid our hearts of woe
Return joy to our mortal beings.
    Show us the Mercy You Have always Shone.

God Heard his plea
>And Saw staving suffering.

Mercy and Wisdom Left their Heavenly Homes and Entered
>The people who again were drawn to God, Their Lodestone.

THE LETTER OF JEREMIAH

In this scroll are words which Jeremiah the prophet sent from Jerusalem to the remnant in exile of the elders, the priests, the prophets, and all the people whom Nebuchadnezzar had carried off into exile from Jerusalem to Babylon. Ep Jer, 1.

O ye exiles, young and old,
    Timid and bold,
Priests, prophets, and ordinary folk,
    All bearing the yoke
Of banishment from Zion,
    No longer shielded by Judah's lion.
You disobeyed God's Laws
    You have heaped high your souls with flaws.
Therefore, God Proclaimed, that you from your land be expelled
    And against your will as captives held .
Be not tempted, in Exile, by an alien way;
    Be not seduced by gods made of clay
Whose veneers are of silver and gold.
    Remove your blindfold!
Their gods have tongues but do not talk;
    They have legs but do not not walk.
Be not lured by temple whores
    Or the impure wine the priestess pours.
Step not inside! The grounds are profaned
    By bat excreta, splattered and stained.
Wild cats run amok running after rabid rats
    And all about them swarm clouds of gnats.
Pens are filled with terrified sheep,
    How they bleat; how they weep.
Their priests sound like raucous hawkers at the souk
    Braying "Fresh sacrificed lamb for you to cook."
Who does a scarecrow scare in a cucumber plot?
    Can a clay god tell you what you aught and aught not?
Is that the way priests should act?
    Such ways you must counteract

> By following God's Sacred Laws
>> And from your souls expunge your flaws.
> Listen to these words of Jeremiah, your friend,
>> And the fragments of your life will surely mend.

BEL AND THE DRAGON: A SATIRE

One day, the king asked Daniel "Why don't you worship Bel?" Daniel replied, "I worship only the Living God, not a god made by man.
Bel, I, 5-7.

"Cyrus, my king," Daniel said.
    "How wise you are and so well bred.
I don't understand why you the bearded Marduk beseech
    When you know he lacks any sound of speech."

Cyrus replied with a twinkle in his eye
    His good friend Daniel to mollify
"Marduk, Bel, Lord of all,
    Did my very soul from my youth enthrall.

"Like a giant he stands
    With powerful hands
That Tiamat subdued in the deepest sea
    And defeated the dragon seated at his knee.

"Marduk, bull of the golden sun,
    With his great powers my people's hearts have won."
Daniel, deep in concentration,
    Told Cyrus it was his imagination.

"Let's put your god through a test.
    Tonight when the priests are at rest
Bring your offerings to lay at his feet
    And we will see if he really does eat."

That night Daniel opened the temple door
    And spread ashes galore upon the floor.
The next day Cyrus saw footprints of the priests
    And nothing was left of the meats and the sweats.

Cyrus gathered the priests at his throne
> And told them that they must for their despicable deceit atone.

Cyrus asked Daniel what is *his* salvation,
> Daniel replied, "The Infinite God of all Creation."

THE HYMN OF AZARIAH

Three youngsters, Hananiah, Mishael, and Azariah, walked in the midst of the flames, singing praises to God. Sg Three, I, 1.

Nebuchadnezzar, a mighty king, demanded the exiles
    Pay homage to his gods.
Three youths, sons of Zion, refused
    And were thrown into a flaming fire.

The heat of the holocaust was hellish
    And they huddled together in safety.
Then Azariah, one of the three, raised his voice and chanted
    Praised be to God, the Creator.
All sang out, "Amen! O Blesse´d God, Merciful Judge,
    To You we confess our sins,
We and our brethren have violated the Sabbath,
    And breached the dietary laws, Amen again!.

Surely You Noticed we have mended our ways
    Surely You Have Seen our devotion
To Your Covenant with Abraham, Isaac, and Israel
    And to Moses Laws given on Sinai. Amen again!"

With contrite hearts and penitent souls
    The three men praised and glorified God
The flames were getting hotter.
    Sparing of breath they cantillated,

"Blesse´d is the Spirit in the waters 'neath the Heavens, AMEN.
    And Blesse´d is the Spirit in the sun and the moon, AMEN.
And Blesse´d is the Spirit in the dew and the rain, AMEN.
    And Blesse´d is the Spirit in the winds, AMEN.

And Blesse´d is the Spirit in the fire and heat, AMEN.
    And Blesse´d is the Spirit in the day and night, AMEN.

And Blesse´d is the Spirit in the frost, snow, and ice. AMEN
    And Blesse´d is the Spirit in the mountains and vales. AMEN.

And Blesse´d is the Spirit in the rivers, seas, and lakes, AMEN.
    And Blesse´d is the Spirit in the fish that swim, AMEN.
And Blesse´d is the Spirit in flying birds and in birds that do not fly.
    AMEN.
    And Blesse´d is the Spirit in the wild beasts and in tame animals.
    AMEN.

And Blesse´d is the Spirit in the righteous, AMEN.
    And Blesse´d is the Spirit in the humble. AMEN.
The Spirit Dwelling in All Creatures Is God. AMEN! AMEN!"
    The Soul of every mortal is Divine. AMEN! AMEN! AMEN!

God Listened to their prayer and Was Contrite;
    God Heard their appeal and Was Merciful.
The Forgiving God then Gathered and Released all of the Spirits
    And the three men were Rescued from the flames.

The Spirit of God Was Dwelled in the trio.
    Hananiah was the Grace of God;
        Misha-el was the Peerless God;
            Azari-ah was the Helpmeet of God,
                God's Mercy endures forever. AMEN! AMEN! AMEN!

THE CONTEST, NO CONTEST

Now when Darius reigned, he made a great feast for all his subjects, and for all his household, and for all the princes of Media and Persia. And when they ate and drank,, and being satisfied had gone home, then Darius the king went into his bedchamber, and slept, and soon after awoke. Then three young guards that watched over the king's body, spoke to each other. Let every one of us form a sentence: he with the sentence that is the wisest, shall be deemed wiser than the others, to him will the king Darius give great gifts. I Esd. 3, 1–5

The Emperor Darius had three bodyguards,
    One said, "brothers
I ask you what in this world
    Is stronger than all of the others?"

Each one an answer sought.
    After much thought
The first guard said, "There is nothing stronger than wine.
    It makes a dull face shine.

Wine makes you reel
    Wine makes you feel
Giddy. Wine makes you fight
    Wine makes you think what's wrong is right.

If wine makes you act this way
    It must be the strongest thing in the world, I say."

The second guard said
    After the king slept in bed.
"Nothing is stronger than the king.
    He rules over land and sea and everything.

He wages war
    He gives orders to kill even more.

He makes people pay taxes.
    At dinner he relaxes

And falls asleep
    Without counting sheep.
We guards watch over him
    And cater to his every whim.
        He must be the strongest thing in the world, I say.
            He is by God Sired unlike mortals like us made of clay.

The third guard who had never been wed,
    "Nothing is more powerful than woman," he said.
She gives birth, she feeds the child;
    She looks at you and you are beguiled.

Her face is pretty; her figure alluring
    Her voice is sweet and truly assuring.
You gape; you stare.
    You forget each care.

With her clever hands she vineyards plants and sews our clothes,
    And in her gentle way upon men she honor bestows.
Her beauty makes the king's heart throb;
    Her charm makes the king's eyes sob.

    Therefore, woman must be the strongest thing in the world I say.
        And her every virtue wine and king outweigh.

Then came Zerubbabel of Davidic stalk
    Whose wisdom brought esteem to the Hebraic flock.
Zerubbabel, of exile born,
    With loyalty to the king foresworn,

Said, "the words each of you spoke have worth
    But what is most powerful on this earth
Is TRUTH. TRUTH is without age.
    It is peerless and without gauge.

TRUTH has no disguise;
    TRUTH despises lies.
TRUTH is Unflawed;
    It is a Gift to us from God.

    In time wine turns sour, kings die, and a woman's beauty fades away.
        But TRUTH Is Eternal and Will forever Stay.
With the words that Zerubbabel expressed
    Was the king profoundly impressed.
He offered Zerubbabel silver and gold
    But Zerubbabel said he had wealth untold.

He was the heir to Moses' Laws and Lore;
    He said he needed nothing more.
He returned to Zion and took the helm
      And became commander of the realm.
        His leadership was so wise, in time, it would galvanize
            The prophets Haggai and Zechariah his flock to Judaize.

THE WORDS OF ESDRAS

And in all things the descendants of David did ungodly things as Adam and all his generations had done. So You Turned over the city into the hands of Your enemies. Do they behave any better than the Children of Israel? When I got to Babylon I saw so more sins than I could tally and my heart failed me. I was vexed because You Tolerate sinners of Babylon but Destroy Your very own people..... And the Angel, Uriel, gave me an answer, And said, you do not know what goes on in this world how can you understand the ways of God, The Most High. Ezra replied Weigh our wickedness now in the balance, and theirs also that inhabit the world. You will find that Israel has kept Your Precepts but the heathen has not. II Esd 3, 26 ff.

By the river of Babylon
    Watching his kinsmen weep
Perplexed, the scribe, Ezra, lamented
    The fate of his people.
There and then sucked
    Into the vortex of a vision
Was he at the Gates of Heaven
    Pleading to be accepted into the Sacred Space.

"Hear me out, O God,
    Alone Divine, Unequaled in Holiness."
The Angel Uriel then Appeared.
    "You need not shout

"God Knows your heart
    And Hears your plea."
Ezra wailed, "We are drowning
    In the dank, dark waters of exile.

"We fret, we are vexed, our souls are addled.
    Do You not Feel our pain? You not Accept our confession?
    Do You not See our suffering?
"Do our sins Grieve You more

Than those of our captors?
Is our pain less worthy of relief
>Than those of our abductors?
'We feel betrayed;
>We feel abandoned.'

"Are we a blight amongst the nations
>Or are we a light? is not my wish to chide You
Or to deride You.

"We are drawn to Your Love
>As a magnet is to a lodestone.
I can't believe that our brutal foe
>Was also Made in Your Image.

"I'd like to be free of war;
>I'd like to know joy once more.
My soul has been stung by a scorpion
>That poisons my soul and perverts my reason.

"Show me Your Mercy and I will partake of It;
>Show me Your Kindness and I will wrap myself in It;
Show me Your Wisdom and I will act more prudently;
>Show me Your Caring and I will enfold Our people in it."

Then the Angel Uriel, Filled with God's Light, Replied,
>"Do you know everything going on in your little world?
God's World is larger. Be patient.
>Right conquers Might but in time.

"How long must a woman wait
>For her baby to come into this world?
Does a heavy rain stop abruptly?
>Does a fire stop burning suddenly?"

Ezra's vision dissolved
    And he still watched his kin keening
By the rivers of Babylon
    But he was lifted into the Light.
As Uriel promised in time
    Ezra and his people returned to Zion
And there their withered right arms
    Grew mightier and more robust
And all were witnesses to God's Glory.

TOBIT, A GOOD MAN, AS SEEN FROM THE EYES OF HIS DOG

For you have taken pity on me: for, behold, I see my son Tobias. And his son went in rejoicing, and told his father the great things that had happened to him in Media. Then Tobit went out to meet his daughter-in-law at the gate of Nineveh, rejoicing and praising God: and all who saw him marveled because he had regained his sight. But Tobias gave thanks in their presence because God Had mercy on him. And when he came near to Sarah his daughter-in-law, he blessed her, saying, you are welcome, daughter: God Be Blessed, which brought you to us, and blessed be your father and your mother. And there was joy among all his kin which were at Nineveh. Tob XI, 15 ff

When I returned from my mission in Medea I curled up on my master's lap.
    He smelled me and tickled my spotted fur;
        I didn't stir even though I wanted to whine
Sympathetically as he sobbed, tears bursting from his eyes like raindrops from the skies,
    Dropping upon my head mixing with road dust caking my skin.
"Kelev,[1] it is you! You have returned!
    "I just whimpered. and thumped my tail.
    "Oh Kelev. You have returned." He repeated.
    I snuggled closer to him.
My paws were raw from having walked in the brambles;
    My stomach ached from having eaten so many field mice.
I limped; I could not digest my food; I needed a bath.
    Still I yapped with great glee when
    The young master, Tobias, like his father, Tobit, a good man, came down the path.

"Father! Father! I am here with Sarah, my bride."
    "Oh that I could see her." The blind Tobit swallowed his words.
"Her beauty wants not to hide from your eyes," Tobias said.

---

1. Dog.

"Father when we were journeying to Medea Kelev ran into the water to refresh himself.
A large fish appeared. He chased it and I caught it. Rafael, our companion,
A master of healing, truly a Healing Angel, told me to cut out the fish's gall bladder
And to apply it to your eyes when we returned."

My master said that only a miracle from God would restore his sight.
And a miracle took place. My master could see again.
For the first time in months he saw light. First it was like a flash of gold radiating from the sun
Scintillating, brilliant, dazzling, enchanting and beguiling.
At that very moment he saw Rafael become one with the light
And mysteriously disappeared. Then Tobit turned to Sarah.
The same grace that dazzled only a moment before burnished her face
And revealed the goodness of her soul and nourished his anguished being.

I had been with him when he was blinded. Assyrian soldiers made a game of murdering Hebrews
And throwing their bodies into the marketplace;
Flies and maggots swarmed about the corpses.
Then some soldiers freed wild wolves who tore up the dead and chewed their flesh.
Could there be a crueler outrage? I could tell when I heard the sniggering of the soldiers
That there was another Hebrew victim.
My master crawled into the market place at night.
As I stood guard he removed each body, stinking with death, and gave it a proper burial.
We returned from this merciful mission late one night.
Not wishing to waken Anna, my mistress, Tobit and I slept side by side in the courtyard.
At dawn birds dropped warm dung upon his eyes
And stole his sight. How he despaired.
How anguished he felt not performing his acts of righteousness.

Blinded, he no longer worked to support his family; he no longer sought to aid the poor.

He no longer felt he was a man.

He prayed to God for healing but no cure came.

Anna, a weaver, supported the family. Soon she became tired, haggard, and ill-tempered.

This saddened my master all the more.

Many years before he had left bags of silver with a kinsman.

Remembering this he sent Tobias to Medea to reclaim them.

His leaving saddened Tobit and Anna.

They feared that Tobias would meet a cruel end.

No one could comfort them; they lay awake imagining horrible scenes.

Tobias assured them that I, Kelev, a dog, and the Stranger, Rafael, would protect him.

They worried nevertheless.

My master listened attentively as I continued my tale.

"We arrived in Ecbatana at the home of a kinsman, Raguel.

His daughter, Sarah, entered the room.

Tobias's face flushed and his legs waxed weak and melted into the floor.

His eyes sparkled and his ears heard songs that no one was singing.

He was in love.

Sarah's heart thumped with excitement; her face flushed, too.

Her eyes sparkled, too, and her ears heard songs that no one was singing.

She was in love.

Tobias asked for Sarah's hand in marriage.

Sarah was frightened because she had been wed seven times before

And each time the groom died before the marriage bed was reached.

The gossip in Ecbatana was that Sarah was a witch inhabited by a demon.

Sarah was despondent. She felt uglier than garbage.

She was bad luck.

She was afraid to wed Tobias:

She loved him too much to let him die.

Rafael Told Tobias to burn the heart and liver of the fish,

> The one that I had chased to the shore, the one whose gall bladder returned your sight.
>
> The aroma of the incense so changed Sarah that she felt she was free of the demon
>
> > And she saw her own beauty as Tobias saw it.
>
> Superbly sublime! She was cured. They wed. The silver was retrieved.
>
> We departed for Nineveh with sheep, camels, and goats.
>
> > Often along the road Sarah would lift me on to her camel
>
> And hold me close to her breast and would rock me to sleep.
>
> > It brought back the memory of how you hid me, a pup, inside your cloak
>
> When the Assyrians sacked Jerusalem and made us walk to Nineveh.
>
> > You shared your rations with me, kept me warm, and clean.
>
> I am the only dog to have been taken into the Diaspora.
>
> > Master, the mistress Sarah is a righteous woman."
>
> In the days that followed Tobit and Sarah walked through the streets of Nineveh
>
> > Feeding the hungry, clothing the poor, sheltering the needy,
>
> And burying the cruelly defiled. In the evening they gave thanks to God
>
> > For allowing them to perform good works,
>
> Each petted my fur as I snuggled close to them.
>
> > The spirit of Rafael Dwelled within them.
> >
> > > As they were healed so did they heal.
>
> And I howled with delight.
>
> > My master had been cured by the fish I caught.
> >
> > My mistress lovingly stroked my back.
> >
> > > And we all thanked God in our own ways.

BEN SIRACH: A GUIDE TO GOOD LIVING

The Torah, the Prophets, and our scholars have given us valuable teachings. Praise be to Israel for the wisdom they provide. All who value learning should be a help to others by what they say and write. That is why my grandfather, Jesus, son of Sirach, devoted his life to reading the Torah and the prophets and the other great works of our ancestors. Sir I, 1 ff.

A Commentary On Ecclesiasticus

1

Grandfather, I would say, Let's take a coconut and play
Or let's swim in the brook "Yes," he would answer handing me his
    book,
Rocking back and forth in his chair, "Child, my treasure, my heir,
We have so much to learn and even more to unlearn.
Help me examine what I wrote and review each and every note.
I want to be exact; I must be understood; I want my lessons to make
    people attain a higher good.
I want them to be better than they now are. Much better by far.
Who first these words did speak: Was it a Babylonian, a Jew, perhaps, a
    Greek?
    I do not know who spoke them originally but they have been
        remolded by me
From fragments I amassed that our ancestors to us have passed.
Remember what the wise Solomon once wrote, and this is the exact
    quote,

"There is nothing new under the sun."

What I have done is taken the wisdom of all ages gathered by prophets
    and by sages
And charted them to unfold a philosophy of life more precious than
    gold
That will bring inspired insight to life-travellers who walk the path of
    right.

Then his voice trailed off and came to a stop- so heavy was the silence I thought it would drop.
After pausing to meditate, his body began to undulate,
And as he was swaying, I heard him praying,
"Lord of the universe from Whom all Good Does Flow Teach us that we may Wisdom know.
You Who are so Generous Grant understanding to us."
Then Simeon ben Yehoshua ben Eleazar ben Sira, my grand dad, grew silent. He forbade
Any talking. Again it was time for meditating, even outdoors the winds were abating.

2

Grandfather now in Egypt I sit translating into Greek your thoughts and wit.
I am doing what you once of me did ask but it has been no easy task
Because even in translating into one's own tongue from which a thought was originally sprung
A part of the essence is lost. There is an even greater cost
When translating into foreign speech the thoughts that one wants to teach.
A meaning in one's place and time changes in another era and clime.
Still your thoughts I will transmit and your God-Given wisdom to posterity will submit.
It will not suffer stagnation but will grow in the minds of each new generation
Who will adapt your messages to the lives they know. Their souls with lambent light will glow.
And their grandchildren and their grandchildren's grandchildren
    And every future generation will have your guide to improve civilization.

3

As if from a dream, grandfather one day awoke and in golden whispers, inspired, he spoke,
"Wisdom was created before all. Wisdom was there before Adam's fall.
Adam had God's Command contradicted and from Paradise had been Evicted.

He paid a heavy price- and how.
> He had to labor by the sweat of his brow.

Eve, his wife, gave birth in pain, and keened when their Cain had his brother slain.

In those primeval days of which I speak God's first mortals were morally weak.

They lacked the burning flame of right and wrong; errant they were not strong.

They did not resist temptation and provoked God's Consternation.

Oh how they did Wisdom shun, dispatching it to oblivion.

They lacked respect for God's Sacred Word and scorned all God's Guides that they ever heard.

Child, Wisdom Comes to all who devoutly worship God and who Creation's Wonders daily laud.

Wisdom Grows from awe of the Lord; Wisdom blossoms when God is adored.

It was mortally wounded whenever people raged; it convulsed and died when wars were waged.

Child! Even when distressed be in no rush to speak; control your passions and never shriek.

Neither hypocritical nor arrogant be; be humble even when you disagree."

Grandfather's energies now spent, he lay down to rest. We continued when he regained his zest.

4

One day grandpa awoke with smiling eyes.
> His ideas pleased him, there was nothing to revise.

"Child, we owe much to Abraham who founded our nation.

 He bought land in Canaan and gave fair compensation.

While others would at God laugh and sneer Abraham's love for God was sincere.

Stored in his heart was each Sacred Thought which to his children he diligently taught.

"Like the stars in the skies will your nation be."

Moses, the teacher, was without peer; to this day we revere that seer.

In this stuttering man the Lord God Saw the one to teach The Sacred Law.
Up a mountain ascended a quavering clod; down a mountain descended the prophet of God
Beaming with light and filled with awe carrying the tablets where inscribed was the law:
The laws he now read to all of Israel and insisted that they be obeyed without fail.

'At all times be aware that there is but one God found everywhere
Whose Name shall never be pronounced in vain or ever spoken with an air of disdain.
Labor six days of every week but on the seventh rest do seek.
Your parents you must always obey and you will never go astray.
Observe the Sabbath and keep it holy; be protective of the lowly.
Never kill another: not a stranger, not a brother.
Do not adultery commit or to passion wantonly submit.
Never steal another's things: whether of the poor or of the kings.
Never falsely accuse; never another abuse.
Respect another's property; lest there be anarchy.'

So many laws did they that day hear; so many laws to which to adhere.
But there were even more to come, many our forbears found burdensome.
But Moses gave each law the very same weight: none was open to any debate.
The message each contains that is today embedded in our brains:
To all people be merciful, just, and fair and of false gods and alien ways always beware."

5

One day I heard grandfather cry, "My mind is squeezed out dry.
My brain is an empty space; my words have fallen out of place."
Then swooping down from out of nowhere was a bird quite rare:
Black with feathers shimmering in the sun Sent to him by The Holy One.
It spoke not a word yet grandfather its every sound had heard.

Then spreading its feathers away it flew and grandfather discovered what he always knew.

The secret of a good life from his mind then sprung and a simple message rolled down his tongue,

"What Aaron, Joshua, and Samuel shared was a nature that showed they cared

For people no matter their estate.
    What was important to them was to consecrate

Oneself to God Immortal- in no way to be likened to any mortal.

This lesson teaches humility. Can the highest degree

Mortals attain be little higher than an ant?
    What cause do they have to be so arrogant

To think that their views must prevail when they measure themselves on a cosmic scale?

Can they mountains grow? Can they make rivers flow?

Can they animals create? Can they life forms mutate?

Humble we must be in what we say. Are not we all just made of clay?

Even with facts we know quite well there is an air of mystery we cannot expel.

The very act of cogitating about Wisdom is elevating.

It is life's supreme mission; it is the mind's nutrition.

Do not relegate it to a lower caste; our ignorance and deviance are unsurpassed.

Those who gained Wisdom have joy unfurled and are already making this a better world."

6

"So many of God's children are truly blessed, but there are others who are distressed:

The widow, the orphan, and the lame, the victims of cruelty wallowing in shame.

They all lack love, shelter, raiment, and food any one of which is a prelude

To disease. And their degradation lowers love of self in their own estimation

And is scorned by those Good Fortune once kissed.

We must plan our lives to give them an assist.
    Sheltering, clothing, and feeding the poor

While not being a cure will provide them comfort so they can rise
And their inborn talents maximize.
And as for the victims of heinous deeds don't cut them down as pesky weeds
But show them all love sincere; everyone by God is Held dear.
What can we do for those depressed, those who feel they are unblessed?
We should stretch out our arms in understanding so their sense of worth will be expanding.
What do acts of mercy do by showing we care?
    We raise the hopes of those in despair.
For acts of kindness like these we change people's destinies.
Such acts of charity will unfetter and makes this world so much better.
Will we receive The Almighty's embrace?
    Will we be crowned with heavenly grace?
When we a cup of mercy have poured the good deed that follows is its own reward.
"Listen to these thoughts that I compiled; listen carefully my love, my child."
It was a sunny day in Spring when Grandfather began to sing
In his resonant baritone, rocking back and forth, oscillating each tone,

"The righteous person is like a tree spreading its branches like a canopy
In season it brings forth tasty fruit. The righteous are so astute
That none of their branches have a withering leaf so strong has been their belief
In Almighty God and so righteous have been the paths they trod.
The upright succeed in whatever they pursue.
But the wicked are like chaff that the wind blows askew."
Those are the images of David, the king whose words will ever cling
To the soul whenever they are spoken.
    They can mend a heart that has been broken.
Those words are like the broomrape plant.
    They attach to your roots and enchant
With their spikes of gold wondrous to behold.

"The Lord is my shepherd I shall not want.

He leadeth me beside still waters and restores my soul."

Mortals will always know grief and will always seek relief.
David planted hope in our souls which in time of grief consoles.
It does not a loss replace- nor tears of sorrow chase-
But each phrase in those lines is like the sun that shines,
Radiating warmth throughout the soul and making us again feel complete, feel whole.
The elegant way David would speak! What mystique
There is in the patter of his meter.
    Can the scent of any word-flower be sweeter?

'The Lord will give strength unto His people and will bless His people with peace.'

After Winter's dreary days, these words are comforting
 Like the flowers that are reborn in the Spring.
David, who to our souls like a gardener tended,
Planted balm which the knives of anguish transcended."

8

"Evil, child, is a disease; it's stench more vile than rotting cheese.
It sickens; it afflicts; it turns good people into derelicts.
The wise Solomon assembled each saying to turn us away from asinine braying
And bring us closer to the Divine and lets us bask in God's Sunshine.

"Listen to what your father and mother tell you.
Their teaching will improve your character.
Resist the immoral person who seduces you with smooth talk.
The Lord Does Not Tolerate a proud look, a lying tongue
Or one who stirs up trouble among friends or family.
Do not be taken in by the charm of a flatterer;
You do need another to gauge your worth.
Honesty can save your life.
The sensible person gathers crops when they are ripe.
Sensible people accept good advice.

Anyone who spreads gossip is a fool.
Never ask a lazy person to do something for you.
Such a person is acid in your mouth and smoke in your eyes.
The righteous speak kindly; the wicked hurt others.
You do yourself a kindness when you yourself are kind."

Each of these sayings of Solomon is a gem, a sparkling jewel in the diadem
Of righteous ways that goodness brings and fear allays.
The luster of each saying is brilliant. It is like a rock resilient
To scratching. It is always catching
Light and reflecting it for all to see. Each is a legacy
From the great minds of the past who for us have these jewels amassed.

9

Grandfather you are so wise. How well you harmonize
Present-day knowledge which is so vast with that of generations past.
"Child, the fragments that have come down through the ages from priests, prophets, and sages
Have by chance coalesced in my mind and have become intertwined
With the virtues taught by ethical titans whom people like you and me enlightens.
My words would be empty without the seer, Elijah.
My sentence, vacant without the prophet, Elisha.
Would I know about justice without the morality of Jeremiah?
Would I know about mercy without the compassion of Isaiah?
Solomon's sons followed not in their father's path and did terrible deeds to incur God's Wrath.
First each son tried to grab as his own the gilded throne
Of Zion and split Judah's lion
Asunder. Is it no wonder
That a glorious nation based on the foundation
Of Torah brighter than the candles of a Menorah
Was snuffed out? Was thrown about?
Solomon's Rehoboam! Solomon's Jeroboam!

The greedy brothers hated one another.
> Each sought to wrest power from the other.

And thus did Israel's North from Judea's South secede.
> What a wretched deed!

They weakened each side. When two brothers collide
In anger each is diminished.
> When the fight continues both are finished.

Mortals must learn to analyze and find ways to compromise
So that we all live in amity and harvest the fruit of harmony."

10

"Grandfather!" I said. "I often hear Isaiah's voice inside of me."
"Of course!" he replied. Isaiah's voice is even inside generations yet to be.
Moses gave us laws. Amos recited our flaws.
But Isaiah who by God was sent taught us all that if we repent
And our ways are no longer depraved- we will be saved.
He is our conscience. He torments
Only when we go astray. So every scheme we must weigh
In order to feel free of sin, of guilt, of shame, and of chagrin.
I hear his sobbing voice proclaiming from the mountain top we have a choice
And pleading with us to scorn temptation.
> God has placed us on probation.

Abhor the Moloch, an idol, a fraud and return to the ways of the Holy God.
Isaiah reminds us of what is right and wrong.
> Listen to him and become morally strong.

Practice the virtues he advocated and to God become reconsecrated.
Then we will achieve the highest state:
> Paradise on earth can be our fate.

We will be with God's glory graced and by the grandeur of God become embraced.
What is clear from what Isaiah has said our destiny is what we have merited.
Never betray God by unseemly deeds and follow only where virtue leads."

11

Grandfather. How can I ill fate not worsen?
    How can I become a better person?
"Child allow these rules within you to preside;
    let these rules always be your guide.
Honor your father with all of your heart;
    sincerely respect your mother who did impart
To you a map with the pathways of the wise.
    With the bereaved agonize;
With the poor their hunger taste; distance yourself from the unchaste.
Do not think ill of those who are old;
    they are wiser than you a thousand fold.
Sin draws a curtain across the light and earns for the sinner the darkness of night.
An acquaintance is not a friend until mutual trust has ripened.
Don't be another's protégée or agree with whatever others say
If their words hurt or if their actions pervert.
God does not forgive the inveterate sinner and in God's eyes you are no winner
If your righteousness you flaunt.
    You must never widows and orphans taunt.
Give them a helping hand. Change the course that you have planned
If it failure brings.
    With your neighbors be friends feuding siblings should make amends.
Crude talk demeans and is no more beautiful than latrines.
The rich cast a spell when they speak even when they with folly wreak
But when the poor speaks a word too often listeners call it absurd.
To defraud the poor is to oppress the oppressed who are already broken and sadly depressed.
Analyze whatever words you hear not on the basis of how the speakers appear
But on their quality and cogency.

Like God show all respect and the vulnerable do protect;
Be merciful and just and righteous people always trust.
Never gossip or repeat a tale; never falsely accuse or do blackmail.
It is often better to silent be than to bite another's reputation like a flee.

If it is not your business do not get involved you will be considered at
> fault and not get absolved.

Never lazy be but show the world your industry.

Do not flatter or give a compliment undeserved;
> be not boastful but be reserved.

Wail and cry when loved ones die.

But there is a time when you must withdraw from gloom and your
> normal life you must resume.

Instruct yourself to be of good cheer and, above all,
> Almighty God revere.

The prophets say,
> 'Do you think God is willing to be honored by spilling

The blood of the first lamb born? Such a ritual does God Scorn.

Ritual slaughter is a human convention, burnt offerings, a human
> invention.

God Seeks a heart that is pure.
> Perfunctory displays of worship you must abjure.

The Lord Takes delight in prayers of the upright;

But not in sacrifices from those who sin and are putrid within.

Good deeds without thought of reward is how we can best revere the
> Lord.

12

After mulling over grandpa's words," I said,
> "By the spirits of the prophets are you visited."

He replied, "the flame of Sinai that burned within Ezekiel, within
> Nahum, Joel, and Daniel

Sheds light on what is pure; and reveals a cure

To the ailing human soul; righteous living is within our own control.

Enoch, a grandchild, too, though not a Hebrew,

Taught that if people transgress they should confess

And ask that God forgive so that a life that is pure they will live.

And who saved the mortals from the flood?
> The gentile, Noah. His soul flows through our blood.

So, my child, we can from everyone something learn;
> never another point of view spurn."

13

"Grandpa," I asked while I was reconciling so many of the thoughts I was compiling,

"Can the many thoughts that you offer be reduced to one?"
"That cannot be done,"

He replied. "Every human has more than one trait. I would confiscate
God-given individuality to engage in such brevity.
Humans are complex; there is no single index
Which can be used to measure them. Although complex each is a gem
That has a sheen such that the world has never before seen.
The luster of People is within you and me and it is everywhere and within generations to be."

14

I asked
"What can I say to generations to come so that *they* can achieve the optimum?"

How wise was his reply, "At all times yourself dignify.
Do not your talents ever debase or your merits ever abase.
These gifts God, The Holy One, has Granted you.
These faculties did God Imbue
In you through Glorious Creation. Any negation brings vexation.
Look in the mirror of your soul; Watch God's Wisdom Unscroll.
See how beautifully you are blessed and in God's Eyes are seen among the best.
Self-reprimands sting; they do not teach you anything.
Certainly not to do better. So self-distrust from yourself unfetter.
There is no excuse to run yourself down; upon self-abasement God Does Frown.
An insult to yourself is a reproach to God.
Upon yourself spare the rod."

Upon yourself at all times be just
And in yourself always have trust.

A TALE OF THE MACCABEES

When Alexander, The Great, was emperor for twelve years he became ill and died. Before his death, he assembled his generals and divided his empire. I Macc I, 8-10; (Years later) The evil ruler Antiochus Epiphanes became king. I Macc I, 20, That king sent decrees throughout his realm that the people should follow customs of the conquerors. They were to treat the Sabbath as any other work day, they were not to make grain or wine offerings, they were forbidden to circumcise sons and were to ignore the Laws of Moses. I Macc I, 41 ff. Mattathias, the priest, said we will not obey the king's decree. He went through the towns crying, "everyone faithful to the covenant follow me...The enemy attacked and killed many, including women and children. I Macc II, 27. Judah, Mattathias son, took charge and battled the foe and triumphed. I Macc II, 35 ff. (Upon his defeat in a different war) Antiochus became despondent, he could not sleep....he remembered the wrongs he had done in Jerusalem (and regretted them). I Macc VI, 9-13

Clash of Cultures

Antiochus had ruled his empire for twenty three years
    When his mirror said he had no peers.
But it also showed Judea, his realm's rough jewel was untamed;
    For this he was dreadfully ashamed.
Wasn't he, said his mirror, a child of Zeus
    Born with the power to break any truce
With Judea, the Hebrew nation,
    Which to the Greeks was an aberration?
How irked he was by Judea's obsolete bent;
    How vexed he was by its flagrant discontent.
After all weren't Greek ways superior and Hebrew ways, inferior?
    His Greeks were schooled in Socrates, Sophocles, Pericles, and Aristophanes,
His Greeks admired the human form and how to navigate a boat in a storm.
    His Greeks knew not only their ancient lore but also the fine art of war.

His Greeks looked down their noses on the Hebrew embrace of the laws of Moses.
    What if the prophets taught morality;
      what if the priests taught spirituality.
The Greeks taught reality. That transcended Hebrew mentality.
    Moreover, Greek gods were visible and the Hebrew God, Invisible.
So Antiochus installed a statue of Zeus at the Temple shrine
    And demanded that priests sacrifice to him the choicest swine.
The high priest said it violated Mosaic law;
    Nicanor, Antiochus's chosen deputy, said that law has a flaw.
The high priest then removed a dagger 'neath his vestment hidden
    And wept, "what I now do is by my conscience forbidden."
He stabbed Nicanor many a time;
    The high priest asked God to Forgive his crime.
When it was learned that Nicanor's blood was spilled
    Antiochus ordered thousands of Hebrews to be killed.
He called on Ares, the Greek god of war,
    To bless his men as he'd done many times before.
A fierce battle broke out, many on both sides died;
    Such is the sequel to regicide.
No Sabbath celebration or circumcision Antiochus insisted;
    The Hebrews with all their spirit these conditions resisted.
The Judeans were by the Greeks daily harassed
    Until arose Judah, a leader of priestly caste.
His voice to Heaven surged and soared,
    "Who is like Thee, O God, Our Lord?"
    Fiercely did his little band fight;
They knew their cause was just, their aim was right.
    They defeated the Greeks with Judah as their guide;
They defeated the Greeks with God at their side.
    After Judah had the Temple regained, he scanned the altar the Greeks had profaned.
His priestly duties were to clean every defiled tureen,
    And to cleanse the sacred ewer
Then to fill the sacred candelabrum with olive oil pure.

Amid great cheer we recall each year

The Holy Temple's rededication at every Chanukah celebration.
With merriment we sing and dance to praise the miracles God daily
> Grants.
From that lamp rededicated, that Chanukah festival initiated,
We kindle the flame each year anew to teach every generation to
> pursue
> The path to free the enslaved who through our deeds will be saved.
Still at times we must *fight* for what our conscience says is right.
> Yet our flame of conscience ever glows through which God's Spirit
> ever Flows.

Antiochus's Last Will and Testament
Into the looking glass Antiochus gazed;
> a curse on your soul his sordid Self appraised.
> He wept as he now with wizen-face viewed his past before him
> race.
He clung to the last strand of life, all alone without child or wife.
> Waves of sadness pummeled his brain as memory brought him to
> the days of his reign
When he looted The Temple and profaned each room and sent innocent children to their doom.
> Oh what gloom visited Antiochus's mind;
> no inner peace could he find.
How many lives were lost? And at what human cost?
> How many lives were cut short in the frenzy of battle sport?
How many bodies had been gored by the thrust of a careless sword?
> And the pain of the wounded and the lame of all of these I carry
> the shame
Into the grave where I'll join the dead and be entombed in disgrace-
> which I dread.
> How callous was I on the Sabbath to attack unarmed victims who
> would not fight back.
And Judah, the brave Maccabee, gathered ordinary citizens to repel
> me.
> Outnumbered, They fought miraculously with resolve and defeated my trained army

In glorious battle that made widows and orphans on each side-
> Oh how kings so often misguide.
>> Now I understand how firm was their stand to fight for the customs which I had banned.
> To defend their land against foreign oppressors who defiled their temple.
>> Cursed aggressors who overwhelmed them in strife and changed the Mosaic way of life.
> As for the turncoats who helped my cause;
>> we exploited each other and deserve no applause.
> Oh Adonai! Oh Zeus! Either One. I am Your son.
> Bring balm to my soul; make my life whole
>> And from my guilt bring release and let me find inner peace.
> But not even one word Antiochus thought was ever heard;
>> And battles flared and no city was spared.
> More dead lay in every street, more wounded stretched out for Death to greet,
>> More ashes were smeared on faces sad; more sackcloth was worn as the world went mad.

Inscribe this in every canon of your lore!
Heavy, heavy is the price of war.

THE MOSAIC TAPESTRY

On a harp each string keeps its own pith, but each tone can be combined with others to make different melodies. That is how it was in those days, when the very elements entered into new combinations. Wis, XIX, 18.

The throng gathered at the base of Mount Sinai
    To hear the words of the learne´d teacher.
Huddled next to one another
    Were the mortals, the immortals, and the as yet unborn.
Gathered side by side were every tribe, race, creed, and nation
    Known to Creation as well as the as yet unheard-of.
Inspired by the Almighty, Moses spoke without a stutter
    As he proclaimed God's Words.
The shell of every word he voiced was Imbued
    With Divine Love, Wisdom, and Justice.

Where have we been? He bade.
    Slaves in Egypt.
Where will be? Free in Judea.
    And next? Exiles.
And after that? In flames and not be consumed.
    And finally? Reborn a sovereign nation of divers peoples
To impart God's Light to the world,
    And to make life Brighter for all now and forever.

What does history teach?
    To hearken to Wisdom's Voice;
To pulsate with Mercy's Heart;
    And to be warmed by the Divine Soul.
"Thou shalt love the Lord, Our God,
    With your heart, with your soul, and with every fiber of your being."
A shiver ran through the crowd
    Yesterday they were harassed,
Today they are oppressed,

  Tomorrow they will be tried!
The teacher went on, "To grow strong, wise, and merciful
  Heed Isaiah's counsel,
Cherish Jeremiah's warnings,
  And fathom Ezekiel's visions.
.

Simeon of Sira's line will teach
  That all wisdom comes from God.
Inviting God into your very essence
  Blesses Creation.
You my people across Space and through Time
  Are heirs to my legacy to humanity:
What is good is gained by working together with mutual respect.
  The crowd avowed, "we will do and we will listen." Amen! Amen!

www.ingramcontent.com/pod-product-compliance
Lightning Source LLC
Chambersburg PA
CBHW071238230426
43668CB00011B/1484